Michael Palin established his reputation with *Monty Python's Flying Circus* and *Ripping Yarns*. His work also includes several films with Monty Python, as well as *The Missionary*, *A Private Function*, an award-winning performance as the hapless Ken in *A Fish Called Wanda* and, more recently, *American Friends* and *Fierce Creatures*. His television credits include two films for the BBC's *Great Railway Journeys*, the plays *East of Ipswich* and *Number 27*, and Alan Bleasdale's *GBH*. He has written books to accompany his five very successful travel series, *Around the World in 80 Days*, *Pole to Pole*, *Full Circle*, *Hemingway Adventure* and *Sahara*, and is also the author of a number of children's stories, the play *The Weekend* and the novel *Hemingway's Chair*. Visit his website at www.palinstravels.co.uk.

Basil Pao began his photographic career in 1980 on his return to Hong Kong after ten years in the United States, where he was an art director for recording companies Atlantic and Polygram in New York, and Warner Music in Los Angeles. His work during that time included the book for the Monty Python film *Life of Brian*, where he first worked with Michael Palin. They have since collaborated on five books based on the travel series *Pole to Pole*, *Full Circle*, *Hemingway Adventure* and *Sahara*. His travel essays and other works, including photographs for Bernardo Bertolucci's *The Last Emperor* and *Little Buddha*, have appeared in publications all over the world.

MICHAEL PALIN
HEMINGWAY ADVENTURE

Photographs by Basil Pao

PHOENIX

Author's Note

Hemingway Adventure was assembled from diaries and notes I kept during, before and after the filming of the television series. It is not, nor is it intended to be, a transcript of the series. The book has a life of its own.

A PHOENIX PAPERBACK

First published in Great Britain in 1999
by Weidenfeld & Nicolson
This paperback edition published in 2000
by Orion

Third impression 2004

Reissued 2003
by Phoenix, an imprint of
Orion Books Ltd,
Orion House, 5 Upper St Martin's Lane,
London WC2H 9EA

Text copyright © Michael Palin 1999
Photographs © Basil Pao 1999

A CIP catalogue record for this book
is available from the British Library.

ISBN 0 75283 706 0

Printed and bound in Great Britain by
Clays Ltd, St Ives plc

www.orionbooks.co.uk

To live in one land is captivitie

John Donne

Contents

Introduction

When I first heard of Ernest Hemingway I was a teenager living in Sheffield, an uncompromising industrial city without a
hint of glamour, until recently, when the demise of its industry
became the subject of a film called *The Full Monty*. A few days
before my thirteenth birthday I was sent to a boarding school
at Shrewsbury. When the time came to take my 'A' level examination in English, Hemingway's *A Farewell to Arms*, *For
Whom the Bell Tolls* and *The Old Man and the Sea* were the
most, indeed only, modern works offered on the course. My
teacher recommended them and, as a taster, I took them with
me on the annual summer holiday to Southwold.

As the grey North Sea rolled on to the wind-swept Suffolk
beach I trudged through the unfamiliar prose, but at night I
couldn't get it out of my mind.

The sense of place, the intensity of smell and sound, the sheer
physical sensation of being taken somewhere else was fresh and
powerful and exhilarating.

I would lie in bed and follow retreating armies down dusty
Italian roads and feel the heat of Spanish squares and stare up
into the wide skies of Castile and sense the cold at night in a
pine forest.

Hemingway's world was close and uncomfortable and itchy
and sweaty and frequently exhausting. It was, I felt, the real
thing. To experience it would require the ability to absorb
a little punishment, it would demand an open mind and a
degree of recklessness. But it could and should be done. This

stuff was too good to be wasted on exams, I must be bold and fearless and go out there and do it for myself.

Unfortunately, in the late 1950s there wasn't much call for provincial English schoolboys to carry mortars up Spanish hillsides, and though I had a goldfish I hadn't fought for seven hours to land it.

So boldness and fearlessness were put on hold and I packed the books into the back of the car and looked out at the Newark Bypass as my father drove us back to Sheffield, holidays over for another year.

But something was different. After reading Hemingway I felt I'd grown up a little. Lost my literary virginity. Books would never be quite the same again.

Life, on the other hand, was just the same.

I passed the exams and never read Hemingway again for nearly thirty years. Then someone gave me a copy of his collected short stories. It took just one of them – 'Hills Like White Elephants' – to bring it all back.

The girl stood up and walked to the end of the station. Across, on the other side, were fields of grain and trees along the banks of the Ebro. Far away, beyond the river, were mountains. The shadow of a cloud moved across the field of grain and she saw the river through the trees.

Nothing more than that. An image, clean and simple, which was to me as intense as opening a window and gulping in the air. And at that moment the phone rang. It was someone from the BBC asking if I would be prepared to take on a new sort of challenge. To travel round the world in eighty days, non-stop, no cheating, no aircraft.

Well, of course it didn't happen *quite* like that, but it is true that from the moment I started out on what became three long television journeys I realised that the pleasure I was getting from often uncomfortable and frustrating adventures was not a million miles from the buzz I had felt on those days on the beach when I first encountered Hemingway's world.

More recently, when it came to writing my novel, who should come muscling his way into it but Ernest Hemingway, and where was it set – in a small town on the Suffolk coast. It was clear that we were on a collision course. For my research I began to read more about him. His letters, his journalism, more short stories, biographies and memoirs and the less fashionable novels. And in everything I read, good, bad and indifferent, the same quality that attracted me thirty-five years before attracted me all over again – the unforced, unsensational, uncomplicated and magical ability to bring the world to life.

And this is how *Hemingway Adventure* was born. His centenary supplied the spur, the BBC and PBS supplied the interest and I finally had the chance to experience those places that had fermented in my imagination for so long.

At the end of it, well, Hemingway's world remains his. Great writing survives because it cannot be replaced, and because the process that created it can never be unpicked and replicated. And anyway, nothing stays the same, not even a mountainside or a pine forest. But I feel I've come closer to him. I have met people he met and travelled the way he travelled. There have been high times: in Venice, and chasing marlin on the Gulf Stream off Havana, and low times: finding the remains of his crashed plane in a small, fly-ridden town in deepest Uganda, or walking through the house at Ketchum where he ended his life; but there was not a day on the road when I didn't think of him, this irascible, egotistical, obdurate figure whose writing had such ability to inspire.

I don't think Ernest Hemingway and I would ever have got along. I don't have the requisite amount of competitive energy.

I don't really care about catching more fish or shooting more ducks or having more wives than anyone else. He didn't have much time for the British and he called London, where I live, 'too noisy and too normal'. And comedy was never his strong point.

Our common ground, other than a fondness for cafés and bars and writing about the weather, would, I like to think, have been a love of adventure. Hemingway was the sort of man who made things happen. He was always making plans and going off to places and coming back and making more plans, and not just for himself but for everyone around him. It was a great ride and very few people managed to hang on all the way. And when it ceased to be an adventure, when he could no longer play the Pied Piper, when other people started to make the plans, he lost interest and quit, in the way he wanted to.

When we started our filming we couldn't believe our luck. An entire collection of Hemingway memorabilia, 275 items from the man's life, including unpublished letters and poems, signed wine-bottles, his Remington typewriter, even one of Ava Gardner's brassières, was to be auctioned in England in the first-ever sale of its kind in the world.

The night before we were to film, we received word that the sale was off. The entire collection had been deemed a forgery.

The sale itself was testimony enough to the enduring interest in all things Hemingway but that it should have been worth someone's time to forge the entire contents is surely confirmation of god-like status.

Michael Palin

CHICAGO/ MICHIGAN

It's mid-afternoon UK time. British Airways Flight 299 is taking me from London to Chicago on the first lap of the Hemingway trail which will, all being well, lead me across the globe from Europe to America and Africa to the Caribbean. We're passing over southern Greenland.

Through breaks in the cloud I can see the polished white tablecloth of glaciers draped over the black spines of mountain ranges. There's a tiny village far below. Find myself wishing Hemingway had been in Greenland, then I'd have to stop and investigate. Unlikely though, he didn't like cold weather. Perhaps that's why he left Chicago. The cluster of houses slips out of sight and ahead there is only ocean and ice.

One of a party of sixth grade schoolchildren is pointing at a photograph of a beatific child with long blond hair and a flowing white dress. 'Who's that girl?'

Her teacher answers patiently. 'That's Ernest Hemingway.'

Number 339 Oak Park Avenue, the birthplace of one of the most uncompromisingly masculine writers of the twentieth century, holds quite a few surprises. Apart from young Ernest in pretty dresses there is the revelation that his voluptuous mother Grace was a songwriter and his craggily handsome father, Clarence, was an amateur taxidermist. But for me, on this very first day of my journey into Hemingway's world, nothing can quite compete with the discovery that Ernest acquired his name and a considerable number of his genes from a man born in Sheffield, England. My own home town.

I owe this frisson of affinity to a man called Ernest Hall who left Sheffield in the mid-nineteenth century to seek his fortune in the United States. He fought in the Civil War and was wounded at Warrensburg, Missouri. He married the daughter of an English sea-captain, and in 1872 they in turn had a daughter, Grace. When she married Clarence Hemingway in 1896 they moved into Hall's house where four of their children were born. The second of them, and the first boy, was given his grandfather's name.

Whilst I get the impression that Hemingway heartily disliked being called Ernest, it's also clear that he was fond of his grandfather who read him stories and instilled in him the importance of manly virtues and outdoor pursuits. Ernest Hall died when Ernest was six, and it was by all accounts a considerable loss. The reason I know all this is that, thanks to the efforts of the Hemingway Foundation of Oak Park,

Grandfather Hall's house lives on and I can stand today, surrounded by American schoolchildren, in the very room in which Ernest Hemingway first drew breath.

It's a rather fussy little room, full of frills and lace, but I'm told it has a profound effect on people. A man from Belarus broke down in tears when he saw it, and an Israeli Hemingway scholar who described herself as 'not a goose bumps type of person' was deeply moved by the thought that, as she put it, 'This is where American literature was changed for ever.'

Maybe this is why there is a living author currently at work in the turreted attic of the house. His name is William Hazelgrove and he's working on a book called *Hemingway's Attic*. It's a bit of a shock to find him there in the gloom.

'I came here to find the ghost of a man who did not grow up on television, a man for whom commerce was a necessary stream, not the flood we find ourselves in now.'

I'm not sure I can take this. Another writer looking for Hemingway, and it's only my first day.

Hemingway was born in the dying months of the nineteenth century and the first sounds he would have heard outside would have been of horses' hooves and not the soft swish of traffic that is pretty much constant today. Inside, he would have become used to the sound of his musically gifted mother composing away in the parlour. She wrote songs like 'Lovely Walloona', a paean to the family retreat on Walloon Lake in north Michigan.

Oh! Lovely Walloona, fairest of all the inland seas,
Oh! Lovely Walloona, ... thy laughing ripples kiss the shore

Hemingway inherited neither his mother's literary style, nor her musical talent. However, his father's and his grandfather's love of nature permeates his birthplace as it permeated his life. There was nothing sentimental about this. Love of animals was not incompatible with hunting and killing them.

'Ernest was taught to shoot by Pa when two and a half and when four, could handle a pistol,' wrote Grace Hemingway on the back of one family photograph. In another, angelic Ernest stands at the end of a happy family group, looking the picture of innocence, hair cut in bangs and dressed like Lord Fauntleroy. You have to look quite carefully to make out the double-barrelled rifle nestling by his side.

As we leave, a group of Hemingway fans from China arrives. They're a little late and they shift around awkwardly at the door, all in dark suits like mourners at a funeral. Two departing visitors are enquiring about the recent announcement of a new range of furniture to be called The Ernest Hemingway Collection, which will include such best-selling lines as the Sun Valley Cocktail Table and the Kilimanjaro Bedside Chest.

It seems it was not just a nine-and-a-half pound boy that was born at 339 Oak Park Avenue, but an industry and, quite possibly, a religion.

Clutching my Hemingway-signed mug I step out into the leafy neighbourhood which he is said to have described as one of wide lawns and narrow minds. The wide lawns may still be there but Oak Park nowadays guards a zealously liberal reputation.

An elderly man offers to show me around.

'I'm a socialist,' he declares proudly. 'My wife has twice shaken hands with Paul Robeson.'

The light is fading as we walk down to the end of Oak Park Avenue. A war memorial which bears Hemingway's name stands in a postage stamp of greenery they call Scoville Street Park.

'That's so crazy,' mutters my grey-haired guide. 'They should rename it Hemingway Park.'

*

Chicago O'Hare. The busiest airport in the world. It doesn't have a lot to do with Hemingway but it's the quickest way to get to north Michigan, which has a lot to do with Hemingway.

He never wrote much about Chicago but he wrote an awful lot about the life and adventures he had during eighteen years of summer vacations at Walloon Lake.

By midday, I've negotiated the long slow check-in lines that are the price we pay for high-speed travel and am twenty-five thousand feet above the grey-green surface of Lake Michigan. The Hemingway family would have taken one of the lake steamers that ran out of Chicago and reached Harbor Springs in thirty-two hours. Today, by jet and rented car, I'm there in four.

Harbor Springs, on the north shore of Little Traverse Bay, is a well-heeled and exclusive small town and the jetty at which lake steamers like *Manitou* or *City of Charlevoix* would have tied up is now occupied by dazzling white private yachts. The old station building from which the Hemingways and all their baggage would have been loaded aboard the train is still there. Except that there is no railway attached to it. And it sells women's clothing.

Looking inside, I have a momentary panic that I've stumbled upon a coven of transvestite train-drivers and that someone looking frighteningly like John Cleese might emerge from the back office, wiping greasy hands on a matching Donna Karan two-piece. This disturbing fantasy is not helped by the fact that the Depot boutique has, alongside the racks of dresses, a perfectly preserved ticket-office, complete with ironwork grille, wooden floor and wood-burning stove.

The railway and the Lake Michigan steamer service enjoyed a symbiotic relationship. In their pre-war heyday they advertised together: 'Upper Michigan – the Charmed Land Of

Hiawatha', 'The Northland's Blue Lakes – Far From Heat And Hay Fever'. But they couldn't fight aeroplanes and automobiles. Once one died, so did the other and the only way to Walloon Lake now is to take the highway through Petoskey, like everyone else.

Petoskey, ten miles around the bay, is the opposite of Harbor Springs. It has railway tracks but no station. The tracks don't lead anywhere but they're relics of a past which Petoskey knows is good for business. Not for nothing was it voted sixteenth Most Beautiful Small Town in America. We're on a BBC budget so we turn our backs reluctantly on the white columns and elegant terraces of the Perry Hotel and put in at the local Best Western.

A television in the lobby is permanently tuned to the weather. A girl with a back-pack is enthusing to the boy at reception.

'You know, I got to see that fantastic sunrise this morning!'

'Oh yeah?'

'Yeah, they replayed it on the Weather Channel.'

We've finally reached the shores of Walloon Lake. A raw and strengthening wind is funnelling down its eight-mile length straight into our faces. This would have been the last lap of the Hemingways' summer odyssey.

Here at Walloon Village they would have unloaded everything from the train that ran from Petoskey onto the steamer that plied the lake.

I unload myself into a tiny aluminium dinghy captained by Strat Peaslee, in his eighties, short, with neatly trimmed silver hair just visible between a jauntily angled nautical cap and the upturned collar of a thick plaid jacket.

Strat's family were summer vacationers here – 'fudgies, they called us' – and he remembers the Hemingways. Dr Hemingway was 'a big man, a hunter'. He once took a bee out of Strat's ear. Strat laughs at the memory. 'He never charged.'

His father was with him, suddenly, in deserted orchards and in new-plowed fields, in thickets, on small hills, or when going through dead grass, whenever splitting wood or hauling water, by grist mills, cider mills and dams and always with open fires.

'Fathers and Sons'

Six miles from the village, on the eastern shore of the western finger of the lake, Strat points to an unassuming green and white cabin set above a narrow beach backed onto a tall screen of pine and hemlock trees. This began life as a twenty- by forty-foot cottage, built in two and a half months, between September and November 1899, and christened by Grace Hemingway 'Windemere', after a location in a novel by Sir Walter Scott. It was gradually enlarged over the years as the Hemingway clan itself was enlarged but it is nowhere near as grand and showy as some of the mansions built around the lake since.

It's still in the family, owned by Hemingway's nephew, Ernie Mainland, who runs an insurance business in Petoskey.

There's no one there today. The jetties have been pulled up, the storm windows are in place and the house has been closed ahead of the long, hard winter when the lake will be ice-bound for six months. I'm quite glad to see it this way. In the silence I can indulge my imagination, try and feel the truth of the many stories that Hemingway wrote about his alter ego, Nick Adams, and how he learned lessons in life among the shores and the streams and the dark woods that surround the lake.

One year, after he'd quarrelled with his mother yet again, Hemingway stayed up here at the end of the season, and after the house was shut up for the winter he went to live with friends in nearby Horton Bay.

One of Hemingway's earliest, boldest and most controversial short stories was written from his Horton Bay experiences. It's called 'Up in Michigan' and its clinical description of the sexual act led Gertrude Stein to deem it unpublishable, his big sister Marcelline to describe it as 'a vulgar, sordid tale' and Bill Smith, one of Ernest's buddies, to suggest he write a sequel called 'Even Further Up in Michigan'.

'Horton's Bay, the town, was only five houses on the main road between Boyne City and Charlevoix,' wrote Hemingway, recalling it from a cold and draughty apartment in Paris, in 1922.

Seventy-six years on it pretty much matches his description. The two-lane blacktop from Charlevoix bridges Horton Creek and curves right, past the 'general store and post office with a high false front' and the 117-year-old Red Fox Inn, close by a grove of basswood and maple trees, old enough for Ernest to have walked beneath them.

We push open the door of the inn to find ourselves in a big front room on whose tables is arranged a dusty selection of Hemingwayana. There is no one there except a boy of maybe nine or ten, who, on seeing us, snaps into a terrific sales spiel covering all the Hemingway connections with Horton Bay and the relevant books in which we might find them – including 'Up in Michigan'. It doesn't come as a complete surprise to find out the boy's name is Ernest. Or that his father, Jim Hartwell, is the son of Vol Hartwell, who taught Hemingway to fish.

The Horton Bay Store next door has a nostalgic Norman Rockwell feel to it – the sort of place where they make TV ads for processed food – and as Betty Kelly makes us coffee I admire her collection of Hemingway photographs and newspaper cuttings. One of them, from the *Detroit News*, reports the return of Hemingway the famous writer to the area in the late forties. He told the paper that no, he wouldn't be visiting Horton Bay. He said it would spoil his memories of the place.

Tonight we eat in a fine restaurant called Andante in Petoskey, whose chef, John Sheets, not only serves excellent fish but catches what he cooks. He agrees to take me out tomorrow for a fishing lesson on Horton Creek.

Before going back to our hotel I take a walk up to the corner of State and Woodland to look at the rooming house where Hemingway stayed in the winter of 1919 and from there I retrace his steps down to the same public library on Mitchell Street where he went most days to read the newspapers. The moon is full and the air is cold, and I feel myself in danger of entering a young Hemingway time warp. Turn in to the Park Garden Café for a night-cap and a dose of present-day reality. Order a beer and settle myself down at the bar. The barman nods approvingly. 'Second seat from the end. That was Hemingway's favourite.'

A scintillating late autumn morning. I'm in a canoe moored up amongst auburn reed beds on the marshy banks of Horton Creek. The wind ruffles stands of aspen sending the sunlight scattering. A dragon-fly settles momentarily on the end of my paddle, ripples spread from an almost imperceptible movement in the water. A soft and seductive sense of timelessness prevails.

Twenty minutes earlier our camera boat overturned, plunging our director, cameraman and his assistant into eighteen inches of water. We're not talking *Titanic* here, but they were in well above their knees and all the footage we've shot so far today has gone soggy.

So, whilst they're off drying out the equipment I'm left, with

John Sheets, chef and fishing mentor, thinking about life and why, despite the undoubted beauty of this place, I'm feeling oddly regretful. For what? Well, not catching a fish for one thing. Although fish are shy in the bright sunlight we have seen a couple of fair-sized steelheads emerge from the shadows but they swam past the bait with almost contemptuous disdain.

The twenty-year-old Hemingway caught sixty-four trout in one day here. Mindful of this I think I tried too hard. I rushed the line into the water, I tugged too sharply, I forgot the loose, controlled sweep of arm and rod and at one point my line stuck somewhere behind John's ear, hooked into the back of his shirt. I find myself guiltily hoping that the film will have been damaged beyond repair by the muddy waters of Horton Creek.

There's also a larger, deeper regret and I think it's to do with that old cliché, lost childhood. Horton Creek remains as it was when Hemingway learnt to fish here, an unspoiled backwater. Its peacefulness and my present enforced inertia remind me, suddenly and quite poignantly, of being very young again, of spending seemingly endless days crouched by the side of a pond in Sheffield collecting stickleback and frog-spawn in a jam jar.

It's ironic that this rush round the world to recapture the spirit of Hemingway should have stirred such an acute memory of days when there was no rush at all.

There's a shout from the bank. The crew return with camera intact, film saved and ready for work. The reverie's over.

Actually, I have a feeling that what brought it on was not so much to do with Horton Creek as waking up this morning and realising that, back in England, my eldest son had turned thirty.

Later. Expedition over. All the fish in Horton Creek are still there.

*

Best Western Motor Inn, Petoskey. Woken by the sound of someone pacing about above me. This is a motel and you expect a certain amount of ambient noise but this goes on for almost three hours, broken only by the occasional sharp ping of bedsprings, and a momentary lull before the pacing starts again.

I find myself unwillingly drawn into all sorts of speculation about the nature of the pacer, ranging from serial somnambulist, to man wondering how to tell wife about girlfriend, man wondering how to tell girlfriend about wife, man wondering how to tell wife *and* girlfriend about garage mechanic, to man preparing to kill us all at breakfast.

The only way that I can curb my hyperactive imagination is to exchange it for someone else's, so I reach for my copy of the Nick Adams stories. I'm struck by the number of times the local Indians feature in them. It's as if Hemingway found something in their way of life that was lacking in his own, something raw and elemental, a direct confrontation with sex and death and pain. Whatever it was, he kept coming back to it.

He was a very tall Indian and had made Nick an ash canoe paddle. He had lived alone in the shack and drank pain killer and walked through the woods alone at night. Many Indians were that way.

'The Indians Moved Away'

People in Petoskey tell me that it was once the largest Indian village in Michigan, but now all that's changed. For a start Indians are not called Indians any more. They're called Native Americans and if I want to see what they do now I should drive north to the Kewadin Casino. It is owned and run by descendants of the tribes Hemingway wrote about.

A ninety-minute drive due north takes us almost to the Canadian border, crossing 'Mighty Mac' – the Mackinac Bridge – an epically graceful suspension bridge which soars above five miles of open water where Lake Michigan meets Lake Huron. It carries Route 75 into what they call the Upper Peninsula and us into a torrential downpour.

Partly because of this we have difficulty finding the place, but when we do I can't imagine how we missed it. Kewadin is much more than a casino, it's a conference centre, hotel and entertainment complex. It moves Basil, our stills photographer, to poetry.

'That is the biggest goddam tepee I ever saw.'

The tall atrium which leads to the gambling rooms is hung with Native American pictures, totem pole carvings, embroidered skins and little devices with holes in the middle called dream-catchers.

'Only good dreams go through the centre,' explains Lisa Dietz, a Native American much concerned with the old traditions. She still tracks moose with her husband, but today is doing duty at the approach to the gambling tables, burning a mixture of sage, sweetgrass and tobacco, which she wafts around with a feather to enhance the spiritual atmosphere. It should be an eagle feather, she confides, but eagle feathers are sacred to the Chippewa Indians and cannot be used in a building where there is alcohol.

And alcohol there is. Beneath an appearance of orthodoxy the Native American culture is happily pragmatic about customers' needs. As well they might be. My guide, Carol, a Chippewa in a pin-stripe suit, says the casino alone turns over 50 million dollars a year to the tribe.

Despite the lousy weather the tills are turning over nicely. And despite a couple of early successes at the roulette wheel, a substantial part of that turn-over seems to be mine.

As we head south on the sodden highway that leads back to the Mackinac Bridge I feel the long ride has been worth it. If only to correct the impression I've been getting that nothing much has changed up here since Hemingway took his vacations in Michigan eighty years ago. Let's face it, there's nothing in the Nick Adams stories that might remotely prepare you for Chippewa croupiers.

My last morning in Michigan. I'm out running early along the shore of Little Traverse Bay which Hemingway reckoned was 'more beautiful than the Bay of Naples'.

Today it's hard to tell as a long white tongue of cloud seems trapped in the inlet, lying low over the water. The gentle slopes surrounding the lake rise clear of the mist and in the soft sunlight the turning leaves of oak and maple and aspen blaze like the last flames of a dying fire.

As we pack our bags I get talking to a couple in the car park.

'We're on the Colour Tour,' they tell me. 'We've waited all year for this.'

Indeed as we drive a meandering but photogenic course toward the airport at Traverse City, the scenic back-roads of north Michigan are full of people looking at trees, swerving with delight at a brazenly scarlet maple, braking ecstatically before a golden grove of birch. It's pretty dangerous, this tree worship.

Stop at a town called Indian River. It has one long main street and looks like most other small towns on the way to somewhere. My eye is caught by a low single-storey building in between Top Shoppe Resort Wear and Hair Creations Inc. It's a hunting store with a large ad for Winchester rifles on the door and puts me in mind of a passage I've just been reading in 'Fathers and Sons'.

Someone has to give you your first gun ... and you have to live where there is game or fish if you are to learn about them, and now, at thirty eight, he loved to fish and to shoot exactly as much as when he first had gone with his father. It was a passion that had never slackened.

Beside the ad for rifles, there is a friendly warning on the door. 'This property is protected by an armed American citizen. (Nothing in here is worth dying for.)'

Inside is a select but comprehensive armoury of rifles, handguns, long-bows with telescopic sights, shells, shot, powder and other life-ending accessories. There's also a fascinating and graphic range of hunting products with names like Gland-U-Lure and Natural Doe in Heat Urine, as well as frankly surreal items such as *A Guide to Successful Turkey Calling* and The Polar Heat Seat complete with provocative instructions, 'Hold Your Hand On Seat – Feel It Start Heating!'

Presiding over this small arsenal is a helpful, soft-spoken man called John who wouldn't have been out of place as a parish priest. He's proud of his business. He sees those who hunt and shoot as protectors of a public environment threatened by private development. The forests of north Michigan, he claims, are being systematically destroyed to provide land for leisure. There are now nineteen golf courses in the immediate area. He and his wife came to north Michigan to get away from urban life only to find it followed them.

He shakes his head. 'We've lost a lot of things we moved up here for.'

I ask what he might recommend for a first-timer and he lovingly selects a double-barrelled Wheatherby with a burr-walnut stock engraved in silver to his own design and by his own hand. It's a handsome well-crafted piece of work which would set me back two thousand dollars. But I'm a foreigner without a licence so he can't sell it to me anyway.

He suggests that if I want some action without the capital investment I should try a gun club if I have time. I tell him I'm on my way back to Chicago and he grins broadly.

'Well, no problem.'

At the end of the summer of 1920, things went sour in north Michigan. Ernest fell out with his mother and never went back to live at Oak Park. He spent a winter in Petoskey and then moved into a tiny apartment he shared with his friend Bill Horne at 1230 North State Street, Chicago.

'It was the kind with a washstand in the corner and a bath down the hall,' Horne recalled. And it's where I'm standing today. Except that the handsome, if slightly run-down row of crumbly sandstone façades where he lived has been sliced in half and the number 1230 now adorns the marquee of a soaring modern apartment block.

Somehow this seems to symbolise the transitory nature of Hemingway's relationship with the city of Chicago. Oak Park was the comfortable, settled, family home, north Michigan the great outdoors where he learnt all sorts of ropes, but Chicago was a way station between home and freedom, youth and adulthood, America and Europe.

In a typical stream of consciousness letter to his fourth wife, Mary, in 1945, Hemingway came as close as he ever did to paying a compliment to the city.

I remember always how exciting it was when I was a kid and the Art Institute where I first saw pictures and made feel truly what they tried to make you feel falsely with religion and the old South State Street whorehouse district … and Hinky Dink's the longest bar in the world … and further back going with my grandfather to the theater in the afternoons … and hot nights along the

lake when I was poor in the summer after the war and the boarding
houses and tenements we used to live in and when had money able
to send out to the chinamens for lovely food.

Chicago today amply fulfils my criterion of a great city, that
is one which becomes more exciting the nearer you get to the
centre.

Here the rolling waves of prosperity on which the city was
rebuilt after the great fire of 1871 are all acknowledged. The pio-
neer tower blocks of the 1890s, full of Gothic detail and chunky
stone-work, stand alongside the sheer glass walls of the 1990s.
It's the oldest modern city I know. Things we take for gran-
ted, like steel frame construction, curtain walling and high-
speed elevators, were pioneered in the city, and the buildings
which pioneered them are still working.

And once in the downtown area I begin to feel the buzz of
the street life which Hemingway celebrated. Just odd things. A
sign above a North State Street diner which reads 'Bad Booze,
Bum Food, Rotten Service, Great Seating'. The constant, precarious presence of the El – The Union Loop Elevated Railway – whose trains rumble raucously over wooden sleepers on a
steel gantry that was first erected over a hundred years ago.
And a woman's voice outside the *Chicago Tribune* building asking loudly, 'So, can your husband achieve partial erection, or no
erection at all?'

I swivel round but there's no one there. It's a moment or two
before I realise the voice is coming from a loudspeaker, broadcasting a radio talk-show from somewhere inside the building.

Following the advice of my friend in Indian River I check
the Chicago Yellow Pages for a gun range. This being the
city of Al Capone, there's quite a choice.

With the help of a latter-day James Bond by the name of

Peter Thomas (futures trader, weapon trainer to the stars, deep-sea diver, etc.) we select a place up by the airport.

It's a gun shop and shooting range combined. The shop appears to be run by two Labrador dogs, one cream, one chocolate, who tumble over each other in vaguely amorous fashion beside a display of holsters and magazine extensions.

There are two people ahead of us, waiting to be served. He is big, and sports Ray-Bans, a pony-tail and a sweat-stained bandanna. She is very big and dressed in black.

Attached to the wall behind the counter are newspaper clippings, with gung-ho headlines like 'Gun Control Wrecked', 'Gun Control Dealt A Blow', 'More Women Packing Pistols'. Some of them look very old.

The wall suddenly reveals itself to be a door from which another very large person waddles out. I feel like Gandhi in here. He appears to be the owner, and approaches the waiting couple.

'Yep?'

'We need ammo and targets. We need four number 9 and four number 2.'

I try to sound equally nonchalant when it's our turn to order but when it comes to targets I'm a bit nonplussed. The owner shows me three black silhouette shapes to choose from. One is that of a hooded gunman, another a thick-set bad guy with oddly creased trousers and the third, unbelievably, is a fat lady.

He lays them out and folds his arms.

'Pick your offender,' he says, without a smile.

I choose the hooded gunman, and he takes me through into a small space at the back of the shop with a stained plaster-board ceiling, a big Coke machine and piles of reading matter ranging from *Shooting Times* to *Handguns Magazine* ('Modernised Hi-Power from Bulgaria'), and the more academic *Firearms Journal*. This last has an advert for a Hemingway bush jacket, and a picture of bearded Ernest clutching a rifle and smiling contentedly. This seems too good to be true. My reason for being here summed up in one advert.

There is a rending crackle of fire from the range next door. A hail of bullets, a grunt of satisfaction then silence. The owner comes through to tell me the second range is ready, and we move through. I'm on my own but it still feels very claustrophobic. Peter has set up the target and appears in the booth with ear protectors and a selection of weapons.

'See which suits you best,' he suggests.

'What do you recommend?' I ask, trying to sound like a contract killer, rather than someone buying toothpaste.

The first gun he shows me is a .22 pistol. I step into the booth and take up position. Front foot forward taking the weight, arms straight, left hand on wrist to steady my aim. Just like the movies. He arms the weapon, calls out a warning and tells me to fire in my own time. Nice and relaxed.

The .22 is easier to handle than I'd expected. It doesn't buck or recoil, and I have to admit I enjoy firing it.

'OK. Now try the .44 Magnum. This is the one Clint Eastwood uses.'

As soon as I fire the Colt I'm aware of a difference. This barks as it shoots. It kicks up, like a snarling dog, and needs some strength to control it.

Peter peers at the silhouette of the masked gunman and nods approvingly.

'Six fives.'

The shots are all grouped around the maximum '5' part of the body. Heart and head.

I think I've been lulled into a false sense of security, for the third weapon, a 12-gauge pump action shotgun, nearly takes my arm off. Nothing slim and elegant about this one. The noise is like a thunderclap and instead of a neat hole, half the target is shredded by the time I'm through my six rounds. The shotgun removes whatever dilettante illusions I might have had about guns. This is brute force.

Though he did precious little writing in Chicago, Hemingway made two very important friends. It was here in 1920 that he began his first real love affair after the unrequited romance with his nurse in Milan (the inspiration for *A Farewell to Arms*).

He met a woman called Hadley Richardson, eight years his senior. He was drawn to her both as attractive woman and uncensorious drinking companion and, according to Hemingway's first biographer, Carlos Baker, she was impressed, among other things, 'by the way Ernest made cigarette smoke pour from his nostrils'. They married in September 1921 and lived briefly in an unglamorous apartment on North Dearborn Street.

Around the same time, Hemingway met and was befriended by a writer called Sherwood Anderson, fresh back from Paris, who persuaded Ernest that the French capital was the only place for an aspiring writer to be. Attitudes to life and art were much more liberal and, because of the post-war exchange rate, it was dirt cheap.

Though it may well have been a desire to escape the close proximity of his mother that counted most in the final decision, Hemingway needed little more encouragement to head for Europe. On 8 December 1921, he and Hadley left New York for Le Havre on the *Leopoldina*.

She was thirty, he was twenty-two. Hemingway's travels had begun. He would be on the move for the rest of his life.

ITALY

Ernest Hemingway had first set foot on foreign soil at Bordeaux, France on 1 June 1918. He had been accepted as a volunteer driver for the American Red Cross Ambulance Service on the Austro-Italian front line. After a few days in Paris, sampling cultural delights like the Folies Bergère, he and his fellow volunteers took the overnight Paris-Lyon Méditerranée Express, across the French Alps and through the Fréjus tunnel to Milan. His train steamed into Garibaldi Station on the morning of 7 June 1918.

'They were watering the street and it smelled of the early morning.'

A Farewell to Arms

Eighty years on, the express from Paris, smooth as a missile, glides noiselessly into Milan Central, the station that was built in the 1930s to replace Garibaldi as the main international terminal. It is a mighty edifice, with soaring galleries, marble walls and classical friezes. If the Romans had ever got around to building a railway station (and, if decadence hadn't intervened, it might have been only a matter of time), this is what it would have looked like. Which was, of course, the intention of Mussolini and his architects who resold the Roman Empire to the Italian people as a symbol of resurgent power and martial glory.

Nowadays, its massive forecourt shelters the very people Mussolini and the Fascists were so anxious to get rid of – foreign immigrants, from Africa, Eastern Europe and, more recently, from Albania and Kosovo.

As a young reporter, Hemingway met Mussolini. He recognised him as an act from quite early on, when he and a crowd of fellow reporters were summoned into Il Duce's black-shirted presence at the Lausanne Conference.

Mussolini sat at his desk reading a book. His face was contorted into the famous frown. He was registering Dictator ... I tiptoed over behind him to see what the book was he was reading with such avid interest. It was a French-English dictionary – held upside down.

Toronto Daily Star, 27 January 1923

The imperial grandeur of the station is now a backdrop for vast and enigmatic black and white ads for Dolce and Gabbana, Versace and Armani – the new emperors. A stuccoed frieze of victorious Roman armies is half-obscured by a Pepsi clock informing us that our millennium has only 332 days, 13 hours and 6 minutes left to run.

Considering it is such a centre of high fashion, Milan is remarkably devoid of architectural beauty. Dajna, a local who is helping us with our filming here, is philosophical. Milan is all about making money, she says. It's in the blood and in the history. The city has never been much concerned with looking good. She points out a group of people gathered around a window peering intently at a television screen. They're not watching football or the latest Madonna video but the rise and fall of share prices.

Yet in the centre of this hard, pragmatic city is one of the most sublimely rich and flamboyant buildings in Europe, the great Gothic cathedral, the Duomo. It's a fairy-tale building, the roof a petrified forest of pinnacles, marble walls covered with three thousand carved statues, of beasts and saints and Popes and every creeping thing. Apart from anything else it's a wonderful feat of story-telling. It's just been restored and has a freshly scrubbed, born-again, pink glow.

The mother of all shopping malls – the Galleria – finished in 1877, and a favourite place for Hemingway to stroll with his first love Agnes von Kurowsky, is still open for business. It stands, immensely tall, with domed and vaulted arcades of tiles and a rich stained-glass roof, from which the designer fell to his death on the day before it opened.

There is an older part of town where red brick takes over from marble and banks give way to clubs and bars and stalls selling jewellery, joss sticks and penis-shaped candles in various life-like colours – green, yellow and midnight blue.

Sea bass ravioli and goose at an excellent old town restaurant, then back to my hotel in bank-land.

Hemingway, still a month off his nineteenth birthday, had a less comfortable introduction to Milan. On his first night in the city he was called out to the scene of an explosion at a munitions factory. The carnage was grim. He found himself picking human remains from the perimeter wire. He used the experience later in a clinically gruesome short story called 'A Natural History of the Dead', in which he admits, uncharacteristically, to being shocked, not so much at the extent of the injuries but at the fact that most of the dead were women.

By my bed tonight is *A Farewell to Arms*, Hemingway's famous story of love and war in Italy. It's an orange and white Penguin paperback edition of 1959, price two shillings and sixpence, which I was issued with at school as part of my 'A' Level English Literature course. It's dog-eared and coming apart at the spine, but I wouldn't part with it. This was the book that introduced me to Hemingway and, in a sense, introduced me to Italy as well.

In *A Moveable Feast*, Hemingway recalled the ambulances he drove on the Austro-Italian battlefront in the summer of 1918:

I remembered how they used to burn out their brakes going down the mountain roads with a full load of wounded and braking in low and finally using the reverse, and how the last ones were driven over the mountainside empty, so they could be replaced by big Fiats with a good H-shift and metal-to-metal brakes.

Their 1999 versions are still made by Fiat, but they are sophisticated affairs with lots of gears and £20,000-worth of equipment in the back alone. Which may account for the nervousness with which the Italian Red Cross has acceded to my request to drive one. I'm sent out to the main depot, given a uniform, and directed to an ambulance. Piero, the regular driver, has a mournful face and a dark beard line. He hasn't had an accident in twenty-five years' driving, and looks at me dubiously, as if the record might be in jeopardy today.

'These Fiats must be pretty tough?' I ask him. I think he takes this the wrong way, for behind the nod of agreement is a hint of anxiety at my motive for asking. The Fiats are fine, he says, but they'd rather have Mercedes. However, they're government funded so they have to buy Italian. We drive around the streets until Piero finds one wide enough, straight enough and empty enough for him to entrust me with the wheel. Empty streets are not easy to find in Milan but we find comparative peace and quiet on the approach roads to San Siro Stadium.

If Central Station was Mussolini's temple for the 1930s then San Siro is Italian football's temple for the 1990s. It's a functional building of enormous size – it seats a hundred thousand spectators – but in its grace and elegance is an outstanding example of the Italian talent for turning engineering into an art form. Piero answers questions about it somewhat tersely whilst giving me instructions on where to go next.

'*Left* here, please! OK, OK, yes, right is good.'

I want to set his mind at rest by telling him that I've driven vehicles under many testing circumstances. Whilst making the Monty Python series I had to drive an E-Type Jaguar through the Scottish countryside whilst dressed as the front half of a pantomime horse. If you can change gear with a hoof you can do anything. But I don't know quite how to phrase this in Italian.

After a while he lets me sound the alarm and press the button that sets off the flashing blue light, which could be very addictive given the swathe of space it immediately opens up in the traffic ahead. And gradually he eases up and we talk about things like his four-year-old son and how he has moved out of Milan because he hates it there and because he wants to be somewhere his boy 'can wake up and see trees'. When we finally say goodbye, he tips me off as to where I can gain a little more Red Cross experience.

This turns out to be a first-aid class at the Maggiore Hospital in the centre of the city, the very same place to which Hemingway was sent for physiotherapy after his injuries at the Austrian front. (The Red Cross hospital in Via Manzoni where he was treated for his wounds and where he fell in love with nurse Agnes von Kurowsky also still exists, but the building is now, surprise, surprise, a bank.)

Tonight's class is devoted to the cause and prevention of cardiac arrest. This is a tricky one for someone whose Italian is confined to ordering pasta, but I nod comprehendingly as we're told how to check pulse, size of pupils, colour of lips and nose. Italian is such a lovely language that even parts of the body sound exciting – like very fast cars or interesting ways to cook veal. When it comes to the particularly mellifluous *respirazione bocca a bocca* I'm aware that the lecturer and everyone in the class is turned towards me, smiling in anticipation. Apparently I've nodded once too often and volunteered myself for a demonstration of mouth-to-mouth resuscitation.

In these hygienically correct days the victim is not one of the blondes attending the course but a unisex polystyrene torso with a pink head, yellow rubber hair and no arms. Even the dummy lips are protected by a square of white gauze which remains stuck to the end of my nose as I straighten up. (Much laughter.)

Worse is to come. I am asked to join two others in showing how to lift an inert body. The instructor appeals to the class for anyone weighing around sixty kilos to be the body. Due to a misunderstanding, a man who is sixty years old but a lot more than sixty kilos is laid on the floor in front of us. I get the middle section. It gives a whole new meaning to bottom of the class.

Still, it's nice to know that after two years of this I could become a fully qualified Red Cross Ambulance Driver.

Hemingway took two days.

We leave Milan today to try and locate the place where Hemingway was wounded. It's complicated because though he portrays his own real injury as the fictional injury sustained by Lieutenant Henry in *A Farewell to Arms*, Hemingway locates the event in a part of the battlefront that he'd never seen – the Isonzo River, now the border between Italy and Slovenia.

This is mountainous, dramatic country, where a milky-green river scours steep, wooded gorges. There was heavy fighting here, but Hemingway never saw any of it. He himself was hit and wounded on the banks of the Piave River in the low, flat farmlands only twenty-five miles from Venice.

The journey out there from Milan is straight and uncomplicated and pretty boring, both road and railway slicing across the rich plains of Lombardy with the snow-capped Alps away to the north a constant, if not always visible, presence.

Romantic cities like Verona, Padua, Vicenza and Venice are nothing more than names on overhead gantries as the autostrada curves to avoid them. Open country is quickly snuffed out by development. The wide plain is in danger of becoming one long industrial estate.

East of Venice the landscape patterns change. Dead straight roads, canals, power cables and the fresh-ploughed furrows of the fields bisect, criss-cross and converge on each other like lines on a Mondrian painting.

We put up at a hotel in Noventa di Piave, a tiny town with the second tallest bell tower in the Véneto outside St Mark's Square, a pizzeria called 'Smack!' and a smoky café where the old men gather to play cards. Eat good plain food washed down with jugs of *prosecco*, the local sparkling white wine, in a busy local restaurant.

Later, before bed, read a few more pages of *A Farewell to Arms* with a keener pleasure than usual, knowing that I am now only one and a half miles from the tiny town of Fossalta, the place where the story was born.

On the afternoon of 7 July 1918, exactly one month after arriving in Italy, Hemingway set off on a bicycle from the farmhouse where he was billeted and rode a mile or so through the village of Fossalta to the Italian front-line trenches where he distributed morale-boosting supplies of chocolates and cigars.

Rumours were rife that an offensive was about to begin and Hemingway, impatient to see some action, returned to the lines that night. He talked the soldiers into letting him move up to a forward listening post beside the river. Half an hour past midnight, just after the offensive had begun, an Austrian mortar shell hit the post. In *A Farewell to Arms*, written ten years later, Hemingway describes the moment of impact:

There was a flash, as when a blast-furnace door is swung open, and a roar that started white and went red and on and on in a rushing wind. I tried to breathe but my breath would not come and I felt myself rush bodily out of myself and out and out and out and all the time bodily in the wind.

One of the men with him had his legs blown off and died from loss of blood. Though some biographers dispute exactly what happened next, it seems that Hemingway dragged the second wounded man back to the trenches, and was hit in the legs by machine-gun fire as he did so. He was taken to the town hall and then to a dressing station at the local school, before being moved by Fiat ambulance (so uncomfortably he vomited) to a field hospital in Treviso and finally back to Milan.

Today I'm going to try to recreate his journey to the trenches and back (without the getting blown up bit) to see what, if anything, is as it was.

A good start. The farmhouse at which he was billeted still exists. It's a long three-storey building standing at right angles to the road on the outskirts of Fossalta. A driveway leads to a pair of mossy stone gate-posts, with no gate, which give on to a friendly overgrown garden. Over a door is a shield embossed with an eagle carrying off a lamb, the coat of arms of the Botter family, who have occupied the house continuously since 1711. It's not difficult to imagine Hemingway, wheeling his bicycle out into the heat of a high summer afternoon, checking one last time that he has everything he needs for the men in the front line.

My bicycle is not quite the one Hemingway would have used, but not far off. It dates back to the 1920s and has been lovingly looked after by a local doctor. The road runs beside deep ditches with bare and spindly trees on either side, over a frozen canal lined with the shrivelled sinews of winter vines, through the forgettable streets of Fossalta and along the sunken road that runs below the embankment. I have to stand on the pedals to pull myself up to the top.

There below me is the Piave River, about 200 feet wide and the water not blue, as Hemingway remembers it, but a milky green, only a shade darker than turquoise.

I can see the bend in the river that Hemingway talks about, but there is a new bridge being built and much of the far bank has been stripped away. The trees that remain are festooned with plastic bags caught on the branches after the last flood. Today the river flows by without much effort, drifting beneath the rickety old pontoon toll-bridge whose days are numbered.

I park my bicycle against a tall black steel slab with an inscription that marks this as the place where Hemingway was wounded. It displays a much more reverential approach to the past than that adopted by Colonel Cantwell, Hemingway's hero in *Across the River and into the Trees*.

The Colonel, no one being in sight, squatted low, and looking across the river from the bank where you could never show your head in daylight, relieved himself in the exact place where he had determined, by triangulation, that he had been badly wounded thirty years before.

'A poor effort,' he said aloud to the river and the river bank that were heavy with autumn quiet and wet from the fall rains. 'But my own.'

He then has his hero bury a ten thousand lire note. The burying of the note is generally considered to be what Hemingway himself did when he came back here in the 1940s. I try a bit of amateur archaeology and see if I can dig around and find it. I get lots of help from the locals, all of it contradictory. The daughter of the man who runs the toll-bridge points me down the slope and nearer the river. The father of the local journalist who has a collection of unexploded First World War shells in his back garden says this is all wrong and it's actually buried at a site further up-river opposite a small island. As I'm scraping around in the sand, a lean and bearded local computer expert points unequivocally to the island itself. It's mid-winter, and though a smudgy sun is reflected off the water, I'm not swimming over there.

Then it occurs to me that if I really want to be true to the precedent set by Hemingway and Colonel Cantwell, I should be burying, not digging.

I look around for something suitable to leave by the banks of the Piave and there in my shoulder bag is the obvious choice.

My contribution to the rich undersoil at Fossalta is the Penguin edition of *A Farewell to Arms*, which helped me to pass my English Literature 'A' Level exam in 1959.

'Chasing yesterdays is a bum show,' Hemingway confided to readers of the *Toronto Daily Star* after visiting Fossalta in 1922.

Hemingway was in his element when writing about war – not what caused it, but how it was fought. No wonder he found battlefields in peacetime such a let down. It must be like finding that your childhood home has become a car park – or the hospital where you first fell in love has become a bank.

Hemingway never flinched from describing the brutality and the destruction of war but he could not write it all off as barbarity. War was a crucible in which something positive could be forged. In battle, acts of loyalty, bravery, and self-sacrifice were everyday occurrences.

I can't help thinking of all this as I climb up the vast terraces of the First World War memorial at Redipuglia, an hour's drive east of Fossalta. Entombed in the hillside below me are the remains of a hundred thousand soldiers of the Italian Third Army who fought and died against the Austrians and Germans in the Great War. It's been estimated that a million were killed on both sides.

At the bottom is a monument to the Duke of Aosta, commander of the Third Army; behind him are five black granite blocks marking the remains of his five generals and behind them, rising up the slope, are twenty-two white limestone terraces, each one a hundred and fifty yards long and twenty feet deep. The remains of those who died are set into the walls of these terraces and the leading edge of each terrace is embossed with the endlessly repeated word '*Presente*'.

It's impossible not to be affected by it. It is as if the Third Army, far from dead and buried, is lined up on parade, each soldier answering his name, '*Presente!*' Each one ready to follow his leaders into battle once again.

It's a con, but a very good one, and it doesn't surprise me to learn that, like Milan Central, this was commissioned by Mussolini, in an attempt to glorify a bloody past and to erase the uncomfortable memories of the massive defeat the Italians suffered at Caporetto in 1917 (and which is the background for *A Farewell to Arms*).

The intention of the Fascist architects is obvious. Anyone climbing these massive terraces soon becomes a mere speck against the stonework, tiny and insignificant before the unifying might of the state.

In an attempt to preserve my sense of identity I retreat to the café at the military museum across the road and order a *cappuccino*.

Music is blaring out, but it's not marching bands. It's Sheryl Crow.

After his formative experiences in the First World War, Hemingway didn't return to Italy for nearly thirty years.

When he did he was no longer the cocky teenager, he was a forty-something best-selling author and international celebrity.

He was particularly susceptible to the attentions of Italian aristocrats and in the winter of 1948 he went shooting at the private reserve of Baron Nanyuki Franchetti. Here history began to repeat itself as, thirty years after his love affair with his nurse in Milan, his attention was caught by the only woman at the shoot, an eighteen-year-old called Adriana Ivancic.

She was wet through and miserable at the end of an unsuccessful day's shooting and after drying her hair found she had nothing to comb it with. Hemingway produced his own comb (by then he was quite vain about his thinning hair), broke it in two and handed half to her.

So began, if not a love affair, certainly an infatuation with Adriana, which led to the writing of probably his worst novel, *Across the River and into the Trees*, which tells the story of an American soldier returning to his old stamping grounds in Italy and falling in love with a nineteen-year-old girl called Renata. The relationship is consummated in a gondola.

In the *New Yorker*, E. B. White parodied the book's style under the title 'Across the Street and into the Grill':

This is my last and best and true and only meal, thought Mr. Pirnie as he descended at noon and swung east on the beat-up sidewalk of Forty-fifth Street. Just ahead of him was the girl from the reception desk. I am a little fleshed up around the crook of the elbow, thought Pirnie, but I commute good.

I'm told that the son of Baron Franchetti still lives in the family palazzo in Venice, and that is where we head for now.

Anyone driving into Venice these days knows that it is a journey bereft of visual delights. It can look sensational from a plane, or from the top of the old tower on the island of Torcello, or even from the steps of the railway station, but if you're in a car you must be prepared to be pushed around the industrial extremities and squeezed over the bridge from Mestre and into the hell of the multi-storey car park at Piazzale Roma, before you catch a glimpse of anything remotely resembling a canal, Grand or otherwise.

On this our first night we make a bee-line, as Hemingway used to, for Harry's Bar.

Now bars can be good or bad but they are always a hundred times better if you know the barman and he knows you. When Ernest Hemingway entered Harry's he was doubtless received by Harry himself, shown to his favourite seat ('They were at their table in the far corner of the bar, where the Colonel had both his flanks covered') and served a double martini without ever having to ask. From those days come the classic Harry's Bar stories, such as that of the elderly customer who, having waited an hour for a table, sat down, heaved a sigh of relief, and declared, 'Now I can die.'

Harry's Bar today is merely busy, full of people trying to be Hemingway. Drinks are pre-mixed and served with a dash of boredom. The room itself is small and, when full, is like an overcrowded cabin on a 1950s liner.

Harry's Bar has become a global brand – a clock on the wall shows 'Harry's Bar time' in Venice, Buenos Aires and New York, and there is a book for sale called *Legends of Harry's Bar*. And that's maybe the problem. Harry's Bar *was* a legend. Now it's a legend that knows it's a legend, and that's very different.

Breakfast at the Gritti Palace. Or, more accurately, breakfast-*time* at the Gritti Palace. Guests at this most exclusive of Venetian hotels are filling their faces in the dining-room whilst we, who have feasted more economically at our hostelry opposite the station, are setting up to shoot on the terrace.

Someone shows me a copy of *Il Gazzettino*, one of two Venetian morning papers, which carries a report of our filming activities up in Fossalta. The Italian language bathes our mundane efforts in a Dante-esque glow. I come out as '*Il cinquanta-cinquenne attore Inglese*'. It may only mean 'fifty-five-year-old English actor', but it makes me sound like the Renaissance.

We are here to recreate the true story of Hemingway sitting on this very terrace forty-five years ago, reading newspaper reports of his death after a plane crash in Africa. I put down *Il Gazzettino* and pick up a copy of the *New York Daily Mirror* for 25 January 1954 with the banner headline: 'Hemingway, Wife, Killed In Air Crash'.

He wasn't killed but he was badly hurt, sustaining injuries to his skull, shoulder, spine, liver and kidneys. As soon as he was well enough to travel he took a boat to Europe and, for the second time in his life, found himself recovering from serious injury in Italy.

Once installed in the best room in the Gritti Palace – first-floor, on the corner, with balconies – he set about his treatment with a vengeance. The treatment consisted of a little luxury and a lot of champagne. But though Hemingway was an expert at recovery, his friend A. E. Hotchner, summoned to see him at the Gritti, could see that this time, things were different.

When I came into his room he was sitting in a chair by the windows, reading, the inevitable white tennis visor (ordered by the dozen from Abercrombie & Fitch) shading his eyes ... What was shocking to me now was how he had aged in the intervening five months ... some of the aura of massiveness seemed to have gone out of him.

It didn't stop Hemingway playing baseball with friends in his room. The ball, a pair of tightly rolled woollen socks, was hit so hard that it smashed clean through one of the windows and out into the street. According to Hotchner, the manager pointed out that no one had ever played baseball in any of the rooms throughout the 300-year-old history of the Gritti. For this reason he had decided 'to reduce Signor Hemingway's bill by ten per cent'.

Baron Franchetti, the man who can tell me more about Hemingway's return to Italy, has agreed to see me. The address is as it should be, a palazzo overlooking the Grand Canal.

Though it has turned cold, and there are ominous reports of the worst winter weather for a decade heading this way, the Venetian sunlight, low and strong, highlights the delicate details on the buildings as we head up the Grand Canal. I've always found Venice absurdly theatrical and today it's more like a stage-set than ever. Above us, figures in eighteenth-century tricorn hats, black cloaks and snow-white face masks are crossing the Accademia Bridge. This is the first day of the two-week carnival, an ancient festival that disappeared for 200 years, before being revived in 1975. Those in full costume are, sadly, a small minority compared to those wearing anoraks, sweat pants and floppy jester hats bought outside the station.

The palace of the Franchettis is approached via a narrow courtyard from which rises the world's smallest elevator, which disgorges the occupant into a cramped passageway, which gives on to a long, gloomy room at the far end of which is a pair of glassed doors which open on to a huge and dazzling panorama of the Grand Canal.

Alberto Franchetti is a slim, slope-shouldered man around my own age. The word languid could have been coined for him. He speaks softly and moves with a feline grace and an unmistakably aristocratic lack of urgency.

I ask him what I should call him. Should it be Signor Franchetti, or perhaps Alberto? He purses his lips gently, as if acknowledging some distant, unspecific pain.

'Perhaps, Barone?' he suggests.

After this opening skirmish he is courteous and helpful. He lights a cigarette and we stand on the balcony and talk about Venice until it's too cold and we have to come in. The Grand Canal has changed, he says, registering distaste. Not one of the hundred or so palazzos along it is still occupied by the family who built it. It's noisy with all the boats and the continuous activity. His mother was the last person to keep her bedroom on the Grand Canal side of the palazzo.

Aware of the short time we have, I try to deflect him from the plight of the nobility and in the direction of Hemingway. He recalls him with faint amusement, protesting regularly that he was only ten at the time.

Hemingway was 'very informal, very American', he tells me. He wore clothes that seemed marvellously exotic to a European war baby, albeit a nobleman's son, flying-jackets and big fur-lined boots and check shirts. He would be totally at ease with the servants and throw his arms round any pretty girl in a way which was unheard-of in structured Italian society.

'He drove around in a limousine. A big Buick! In that time, no one in Italy, not even Giovanni Agnelli [the head of Fiat] drove around in a limousine.'

The Barone pauses, leans forward, extinguishes his cigarette and speaks with soft intensity.

'He lived the legend, you see, he lived the legend.'

After an hour together we not only part on Michael and Alberto terms but he has invited us to come to the last duck-shoot of the season and see for ourselves what Hemingway liked so much about this particularly Venetian activity. He impresses upon me that duck-shooting is a serious business, with rituals and traditions stretching back five centuries. Its rules and regulations are essentially feudal, rural and zealously observed. Shooting takes place at dawn but the preparations begin the night before. I am given an address, driving instructions, and warned to bring very warm clothing, and a jacket and tie. Oh, and no girlfriends, it's male only.

We find ourselves driving once again across the flat, grid-like scenery east of Venice, beyond the Piave, and across the Livenza, before turning off the autostrada towards the town of Cáorle on the Adriatic coast.

Just before the town we turn into a narrow road which becomes a track which follows a network of irrigation ditches through an increasingly deserted agricultural landscape until it fetches up at a gabled, red-brick two-storey building that looks like a country railway station. This is the *casone*, the hunting lodge, at which the shooting party will soon assemble.

Before we left Venice the Barone briefed me about the formalities. Guests arrive around seven in the evening, drink and talk until it's time to eat and drink, then, after eating and drinking, gather around an open log fire to play card games, tell jokes and drink. After that there are late-night drinks followed by various manly pranks, like making apple-pie beds for fellow guests, followed by maybe two hours' oblivion before being woken at four for breakfast. After the morning shoot, the party returns to the *casone* to eat and drink before going home.

I am the first guest to arrive. The staff flit about adjusting, preparing and table-laying. I nose around. The buildings have been quite extensively tarted up in reproduction rustic style with shiny new brick and timber-clad walls on which hang old prints of hunters at work or lovingly painted depictions of the various kinds of duck they kill. The gun-rack in the hallway is predictable but not the stuffed black bear (shot in

Romania) that rears up at the bottom of the stairs, nor the leopard skin stretched across one wall. I learn later that these were both victims of Alberto's father, Nanyuki, who used to own this lodge and estate.

Car wheels crunch on the gravel outside and the guests begin to assemble. They are not as intimidatingly correct as I had feared, in fact our host is not a nobleman but a chicken millionaire from Vicenza.

There are ten of us for dinner and we barely fill half the great oak dining table. We eat by candlelight. All three courses are fish – apparently, it is not good luck to serve red meat before a shoot. Everything is locally caught and absolutely fresh, my host assures me, apart from the prawns which turn out to be from the USA. (They're actually a lot more palatable than the rubbery local squid which defy all attempts at mastication.) The sea-food risotto and the local eel and gilt-head are beautifully prepared and Pinot Grigio is liberally poured. A local millionaire called Giuseppe, who has in his time shot everything, including polar bear, waxes wonderfully indignant about the Green movement and is apoplectic about our own royal consort.

'Prince Philip,' he shouts, veins bulging, banging the table, 'head of World Wildlife Fund, kills two hundred pheasant in a day!'

By midnight the party is beginning to break up and some people are actually talking of going home before tomorrow's shoot.

Alberto seems regretful.

'There used to be some fun when everyone stayed here, eels in the bed, naughty pictures upstairs. No women,' he adds wistfully.

'No women at all.'

*

Up before dawn. It is bitterly, bitterly cold, but the skies are clear and the stars abundant.

Slip a copy of *Across the River and into the Trees* into my pocket, for Hemingway's descriptions of a duck-shoot on the frozen lagoon are amongst his most unforgettable images.

Outside the *casone* the flat-bottomed boats are ready for the hunters. I'm to shoot with Alberto, though not literally, as I'm very fond of ducks and anyway the hunting party would surely not appreciate a novice in such a serious endeavour. Alberto shrugs. 'Hemingway did not take it so seriously. He would bring a book to read and a bottle of whisky.'

Well, now I don't feel so bad. Alberto checks his Beretta 12-gauge shotgun one last time and we clamber into the boat. A flock of wooden decoy ducks is gathered in the bows, and our boatman sits in the stern with his dog, which will later retrieve the fallen ducks.

'*In bocca al lupo!*' they shout to each other. For an alarming moment I think they may be calling for mouth-to-mouth resuscitation. In fact it means 'In the mouth of the wolf,' the traditional duck-shooters' equivalent of the actors' 'Break a leg!'

Our boats set out in convoy, through the tall grass of the marshes, towards the lakes where our hides are located. This lagoon area, called the Valle, was created and laid out for private duck-shooting and, unlike much of the Véneto, it remains unencroached, wild and mysterious.

As the sun comes up we can see the snow-covered flanks of Monte Cavallo, fifty or sixty miles north, bathed in the rich pink glow of dawn. This makes Alberto uncomfortable. The air is too still, too clear. Duck-shooting is best done in foul weather when the wind out at sea drives the ducks back inland, over the lagoon.

Meanwhile the boatmen are standing and heaving on their

oars. I can see Hemingway's words in *Across the River* spring-ing to life.

It was all ice, new-frozen during the sudden, windless cold of the night. It was rubbery and bending against the thrust of the boat-man's oar.

I'd never been that comfortable with 'rubbery' ice, but this morning I can see how well the metaphor works. The new ice does indeed bend and flex, clinging on to the oar as it enters the water and sticking to it as it leaves.

Having secured footage of oars and keels and picturesquely cracking ice, the director is happy and the boatmen are able to ship their oars and pull the outboards into life. I can see this pains a traditionalist like the Barone.

'Motor-boats only came in the late sixties, you know.' A smile flickers at the corner of his mouth. 'Of course we all thought it was the end of the world. Like we did when the electricity pylons came in the fifties.'

After about half an hour the narrow channel broadens into a lake, in the middle of which is a tiny artificial island with two plastic barrels sunk into it. Each one is around four and a half feet deep and allows room for the swivel-seat shooting stools.

Alberto and I are put ashore and lower ourselves into our respective barrels. Our boatman throws the decoys into the water beside us then reaches into a cage and produces a num-ber of real ducks which he drops unceremoniously overboard. These are the *vivi*, live ducks, tethered in the water, whose plaintive quacks will hopefully attract their over-flying col-leagues within range of Alberto's Beretta.

Alberto is no mean gun – only last week he bagged forty or more. But today things are slow, and he produces his duck-whistle to augment the cries of the *vivi*. Though it looks deceptively simple the whistle can, in the hands of an expert, produce all sorts of different sounds for the different breeds.

All we need now are the ducks. Everything else flies over – geese, swans, cormorant, but the ducks are giving us a wide berth. The one promising flock swings round and heads up from the south towards us.

'Get down!' cries Alberto. But the flock veers away at the last minute. 'Probably mallard,' comes Alberto's disappointed voice from the barrel next to me.

Apparently mallard, being a native of these parts, are canny and used to hunters, whereas other ducks, from the sticks of Eastern Europe, passing over on their annual migration to the lakes of Central Africa, are less likely to suspect the presence of men pretending to be small islands.

As time passes, Alberto tends to embellish the qualities of his adversary – 'Ducks are very intelligent, they see and hear well' – at the expense of his own species: 'Who is that by the camera wearing a red jacket? ... Who is that idiot standing up?' But most wounding of all is that the chicken millionaire in a nearby barrel has bagged four already.

'His ducks are calling well,' admits Alberto.

Certainly our *vivi*, having got over their initial indignation at being thrown in the water, seem to be quite happy, dipping for fish and not attracting anyone.

So we wait and call and wait and watch. Alberto turns out to be a good companion, and his wide and sympathetic knowledge of country matters bears out the point that no one knows or cares more about the habits of animals than those who kill them. I learn, for instance, that if the female of a pair of ducks is shot, the male will always come back to look for her, whereas a female will never come back for a male.

Alberto likes me because I'm not impatient. I don't like to tell him that I have followed Hemingway's example and brought a book to read, as well as a hip-flask. And opened both.

After an hour and a half there is sudden excitement. A flock is turning towards us, only fifty yards away and coming in low. To encourage them, Alberto is frantically giving his widgeon on the whistle. Then, just as they seem to be taking avoiding action, I hear a shot followed by the thwack of a bird skidding across the ice. A spent cartridge flies out of the magazine, narrowly missing my left ear. Alberto looks relieved. The duck flaps for a while and lies still.

And that's all we get. Though we remain in the barrels for a hopeful half-hour more, it seems the curse of Palin, that so frustrated our trout-fishing in Michigan, has struck again.

Back at the *casone* the mood is subdued. No one in the party even shot double figures. Various theories are advanced. Weather too settled, end of the season, so ducks wiser. Alberto tries to make us feel better.

'Hemingway was not so good, you know.' He peels off a balaclava, smooths his hair back and goes on. 'At the end of the shoot, all the ducks would be arranged in the yard in front of the house, so everyone could see what everyone had caught. And it was a little embarrassing sometimes, because someone would have sixty, another fifty, and Hemingway only four.'

'Four?'

Alberto nods, and I detect a hint of barely suppressed satisfaction. 'He was not a good shot but he was a great character.'

The newspapers this morning lead with stories of unheard-of weather conditions. Winds from Siberia, snow in Sicily.

Oddly, the worst weather is in the south. Perhaps it's too cold to snow up here. Instead we have bright, crisp sunshine as our train pulls out through the straggling northern suburbs of Milan, heading for the lakes and the mountains.

Italy has been a revelation. I have seen where Hemingway shot and was shot at. I've drunk in his bars and sat in his hotel. I have walked the cities where he fell in love. I've seen where the legend of the warrior began and met those who saw the start of his final decline.

But that is to jump ahead.

When Hemingway first left Italy he was nineteen. *A Farewell to Arms* would not be written for another ten years. He was, however, already somebody special. He had been to war, he had recovered from a bomb blast that had left 227 separate wounds in his legs and he would go back to America as a war hero. 'Worst Shot-Up Man in US Returns Home' shouted the *Chicago American* as he arrived in New York. The beautiful woman who'd nursed him was in love with him and the Italians had given him a medal. And all because he had followed his own gut instinct, made his own moves, wriggled out of the loving, stifling grasp of his family.

He tried to adjust to life back home, but once the war-hero adulation had worn off and his beautiful nurse had written to tell him she'd found someone else, the old frustration set in.

The next time Hemingway left for Europe it was not six months but nine years before he came back to live in America.

Sudden blackness. Into the tunnel and under the Alps. We shall be in Paris in another four hours.

PARIS

'Then there was the bad weather.'

This is how Hemingway begins *A Moveable Feast* – his fond tribute to one of the world's most beautiful cities. And it gets worse. In the sort of paragraph which puts travel agents out of business, he waxes lyrical over 'the smell of dirty bodies', 'a sad, evilly run café where the drunkards of the quarter crowded together', and leaves lying 'sodden in the rain'.

From such uncompromising beginnings Hemingway fashions one of the most tasty, tantalising and original glimpses of the city of Paris, without once having to resort to the word 'romantic'.

The irony is that a book which celebrates the promise of a young man with a life ahead of him was completed in the year Hemingway killed himself and published after his death.

A Moveable Feast is a bittersweet legacy, but amongst the bitterness (directed almost entirely at those who were once his friends) is a fine *evocation of what it was like to be young and starting out on an awfully big adventure. How much of it still rings true remains to be seen.*

As we unload our filming equipment outside a hotel in the rue Delambre on this fading February afternoon there is one thing he was absolutely right about. The weather is lousy.

Our hotel is in the heart of Montparnasse where Hemingway sites are as frequent as the trees on the street. Almost anywhere Ernest blew his nose qualifies for a mention in one or other of the guidebooks.

I decide this first morning to take an early orientation course, a Hemingway trail of my own. Trying to plan it on a map is like one of those children's puzzles where you have to join up the dots to make a donkey so I give that up and simply turn right out of the hotel and head for the nearest breakfast.

This being Paris, the first place of refreshment is about twenty yards away.

Disconcertingly though, it's Italian. Even more disconcertingly it's called the Auberge de Venise, and its walls are decorated with gondolas and palazzos and views of the Grand Canal. I half expect to see Barone Franchetti lighting up on one of the balconies.

In fact this espresso-fragrant establishment ties together Hemingway's Venice and Hemingway's Paris rather neatly, for this was once the Dingo Bar, and it was here that Ernest first met Scott Fitzgerald.

He had come into the Dingo Bar in the Rue Delambre where I was sitting with some completely worthless characters, had introduced himself and introduced a tall pleasant man who was with him as Dunc Chaplin, the famous pitcher. I had not followed Princeton baseball and had never heard of Dunc Chaplin but he was extraordinarily nice, unworried, relaxed and friendly and I much preferred him to Scott.

A Moveable Feast

I dip my biscuit into the *cappuccino* and shut my eyes and try to engineer some psychic link-up between myself and two of the most celebrated American authors of the century – and Dunc, of course – but all I get is the bronchial roar of the coffee machine and a request to move up as the place is getting busy and I've been here twenty minutes.

Other ghosts linger in the Auberge de Venise a.k.a. the Dingo Bar. Hemingway used to drink here with an English aristocrat called Lady Duff Twysden (born Dorothy Smurthwaite) and her lover Pat Guthrie. They became his models for Brett Ashley, one of the best, least sentimental of Hemingway's female creations, and Mike Campbell in *The Sun Also Rises*. Maybe these were the worthless characters he was referring to.

A couple of doors down the street was the publisher of a remarkable book called *Kiki's Memoirs*, the saucy reminiscences of the lover of Man Ray, illustrated with her own drawings and copious nude photographs. Hemingway was persuaded to write an introduction to the book (something he did very rarely). Disguised in his playful anti-grammatical style was a sharp epitaph on the life that had once drawn him to these busy streets.

Kiki became monumental and Montparnasse became rich, prosperous, brightly lighted, dancinged, shredded-wheated, grapenuts-ed or grapenutted (take your choice, gentlemen, we have all these breakfast foods now) and they sold caviar at the Dôme, well, the Era for what it was worth, and personally I don't think it was worth much, was over.

That was written in 1929. By then Paris had gone sour for Hemingway. Many of his friends were alienated by their portrayals in *The Sun Also Rises*, and his own output had become bogged down by a novel, provisionally titled *Jimmy Breen*, which was never to be published.

Eight years earlier it was all optimism, and as I turn out of the rue Delambre and leave behind the celebrated cafés of

Montparnasse – the Rotonde, Select and the Dôme, I find myself in a place where Hemingway seemed unequivocally happy, the Jardin du Luxembourg, where in the winter 'the trees were sculpture without their leaves', and the fountains still blow in the bright light. Hemingway had so little money in those early years that he used to walk through here to avoid passing restaurants or cafés. Like much of the central area of Paris, it still seems anchored in the past.

I can reasonably believe, then, that Hemingway would have seen pretty much what I see around me as I walk the neatly brushed gravel paths, out of the western gate of the Jardin through a formidable girdle of black iron railings, across the rue Guynemer and run the gauntlet of six-storey apartment blocks that flank both sides of the rue de Fleurus. He would have stopped most times at Number 27, for this is where Gertrude Stein lived.

She was one of the contacts that Sherwood Anderson had given Hemingway when he left the USA for Paris just before Christmas 1921, and she proved to be the most influential. They became good friends and she provided him with the fresh, invigorating, modern ideas about art and life that he had never found in Oak Park. She encouraged a style of writing that relied less on traditional syntax and fluent, fully rounded sentences and more on the overall feel and emotion of language. (Not everyone was as taken with it as Hemingway. The writer Wyndham Lewis called it her 'infantile, dull-witted, dreamy stutter'.) Literature, she felt, could learn from art and something like Cézanne's technique of painstakingly applied repetition of line and brushstroke to build up an image could be applied to the written word.

'He wanted to write like Cézanne painted,' Hemingway has his alter ego, Nick Adams, saying in a short story called 'On Writing'.

He took Stein seriously as a teacher (though he did tell Hadley, his wife, that he thought her breasts 'must have weighed ten pounds apiece') and she took him seriously as a writer, encouraging him to give up the journalism that was paying his way in Paris and concentrate on fiction.

It was Gertrude Stein who recommended he go to see bullfighting in Spain and taught him to cut his wife's hair. It was at her soirées that he met writers like James Joyce and D. H. Lawrence, and artists like Picasso and Juan Gris. But she paid scant attention to Hadley, and the relentless championing of her husband may have contributed to the tensions that broke up the Hemingways' marriage four years after they arrived in Paris.

I try to ignore the February drizzle as I walk, early on a Saturday morning, along one of the streets, huddled in by apartment buildings, that runs up the hill from Notre Dame and the River Seine to the once poor and anonymous area which was the Hemingways' first permanent address in Paris.

Thanks to *A Moveable Feast* we know quite a bit about their home at 74 rue du Cardinal Lemoine. We know it was on the third floor, and was what they called a cold-water flat, with a squat toilet outside on the landing. This was not connected to a main drainage system and the sewage had to be pumped into a horse-drawn tank and taken away. Coal-dust bricks called *boulets* had to be carried up the stairs for heating and cooking. It had a view on to cobbled streets along which goats were led by a goatherd with a pipe, with which he alerted those wanting fresh milk.

There are no cobbles any more on the rue du Cardinal Lemoine, or goats, as far as I can see, but the tall, plain murky white façade of Number 74 is still there. It's no longer anony-

CHICAGO / MICHIGAN

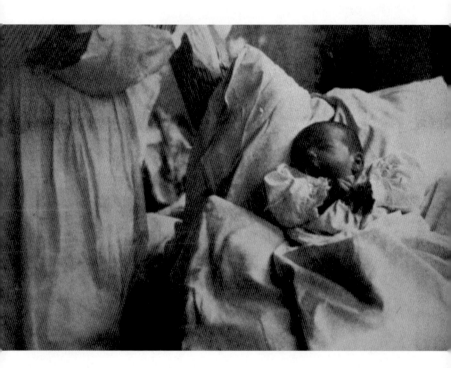

LEFT: 'Who's that girl?'
Early photos of young Ernest
confuse visitors at his
birthplace.
BELOW: Ernest Hall,
Sheffield-born grandfather
of Ernest (with weapon),
Ursula and Marcelline.
OPPOSITE ABOVE: The front
of 339 Oak Park Avenue looks
naked with its porch removed
for Hemingway centenary
restoration.
OPPOSITE BELOW: Marcelline,
Madelaine, Clarence, Grace,
Ursula and Ernest (still to
come, Carol and Leicester).
Oak Park 1906.

LEFT: The public library on Mitchell Street, Petoskey. Here in 1919 Hemingway read the papers, borrowed books and gave speeches about his war experiences to delighted female audiences.

ABOVE: Windemere, the Hemingway holiday home today.
LEFT: Horton Bay, Michigan, inspiration for Hemingway's earliest published stories and very little changed.

ABOVE: Crossing the Chicago River, leaving behind the glossy corporate skyscrapers on the less than glossy train to Oak Park.

LEFT: Ernest and his first wife, Hadley Richardson. He was twenty-two when they married, twenty-eight when they divorced in Paris.

OPPOSITE TOP RIGHT: Kewadin Casino, Sault Sainte Marie, Michigan – which earns 50 million dollars a year for the Chippewa tribe.

OPPOSITE CENTRE: At a gun shop in rural Michigan I test drive a Wheatherby double-barrelled over and under muzzle-loader and try to pretend I know what that all means. The array of weapons is fearsome, the people who sell them quite the opposite.

OPPOSITE BELOW: Picture postcard time. On Horton Creek, one of the shallow streams of north Michigan, Hemingway perfected his fishing technique (opposite top left) and Palin abandoned his. You can almost hear the steelhead trout sighing with relief as my canoe comes towards them.

OVERLEAF: The oldest modern city in the world. Chicago at sunset from the ninety-sixth floor of the Hancock Center.

ITALY

TOP: Milan Central, my gateway to north Italy. Completed in 1931, with a 700-foot-long concourse that's more like a cathedral. Décor is Art Nouveau with Fascist triumphalism thrown in.

ABOVE: Winged horses and mighty human athletes decorate the front of the station. On his first night young Hemingway (opposite above) walked beneath the soaring glass roof of the Galleria – the world's first great shopping mall (right).

OPPOSITE FAR RIGHT: Many subsequent nights, recovering after his injury, were spent falling in love with his American nurse, one of the few women known to have jilted Ernest.

OPPOSITE BELOW: The wounded hero, Milan 1918.

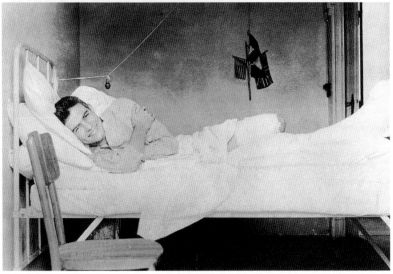

RIGHT: The Piave river at Fossalta. The Italian positions were on the left bank, Austrian on the right, when battle began at midnight on 8 July 1918.
BELOW: Hemingway borrowed a bicycle to take him up to the front line. He would have travelled roads like these.

RIGHT & OPPOSITE: Redipuglia. Mussolini made sure the First World War dead would not be forgotten with a memorial that takes up an entire hillside. The memorial commemorates over a hundred thousand Italians killed on the Eastern front in the First World War.

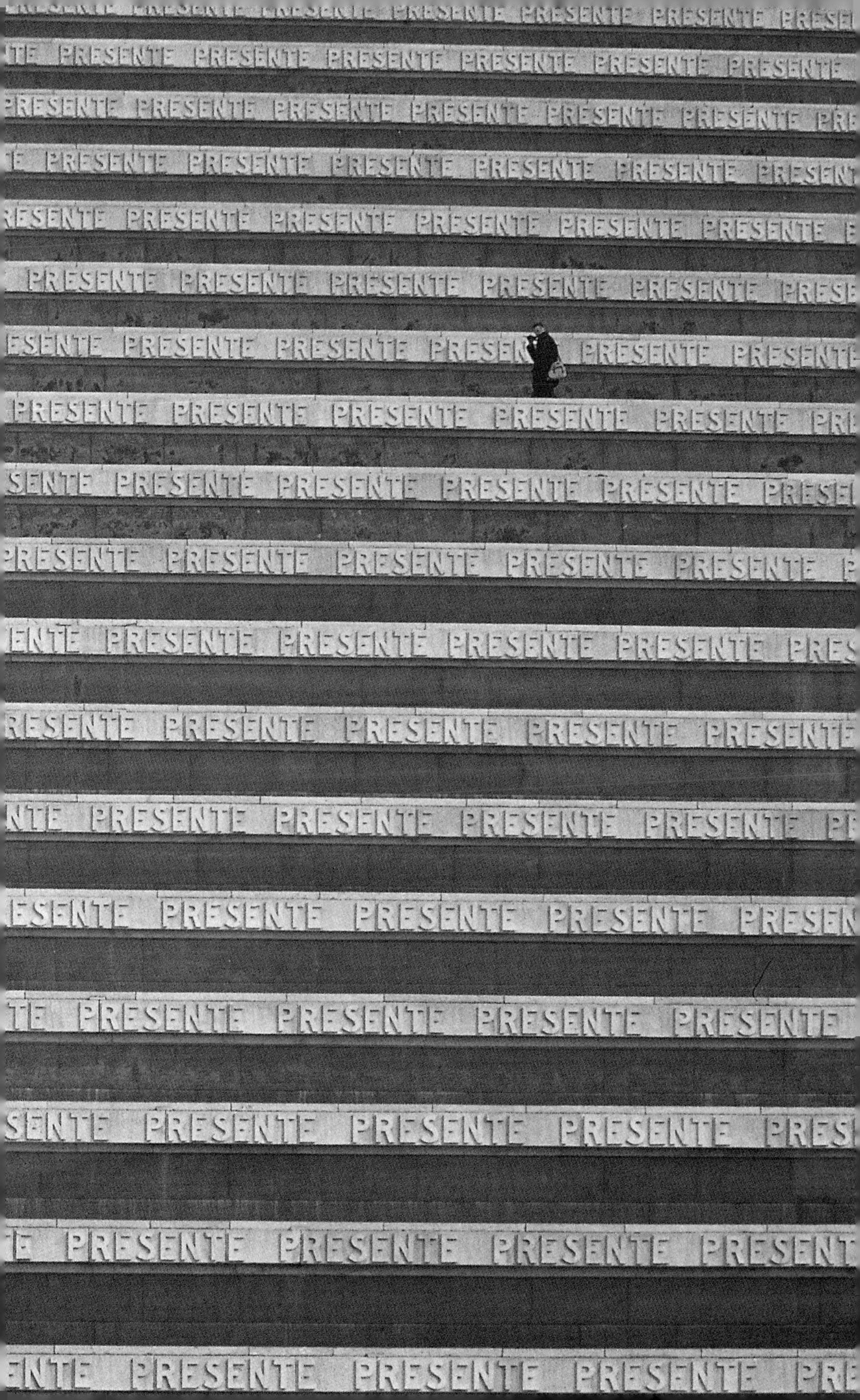
PRESENTE

TOP: Venice carnival in full swing in St Mark's Square. Masks traditionally disguise social differences and serious celebrants order theirs a year early. In 1646 diarist John Evelyn described it as 'folly and madness'.

ABOVE: The Old Man and the Mask.

LEFT: Barone Alberto Franchetti looking out from his family palazzo on the Grand Canal, where parking (opposite top) is a problem at carnival time.

CENTRE & BELOW: Duck-shooting in the marshes east of Venice. Clear skies and frozen water as we leave the hunting lodge at first light. Later in a barrel with the Barone. Most ducks ignored us.
OVERLEAF: A farmhouse in the flatlands of the Piave valley at Fossalta.

PARIS

ABOVE & OPPOSITE: An apartment near the rue Mouffetard was Ernest and Hadley Hemingway's first real home in Paris in 1922. LEFT: Hemingway's passport. BELOW: The Lost Generation: Hemingway and the circle of ex-pat friends he immortalised in *The Sun Also Rises*.

No 359666

TOP: Shakespeare and Company, Valhalla for book lovers. George Whitman believes in total literary immersion, including sleeping accommodation amongst the shelves, Sunday tea and Christmas Day opening.
ABOVE: La Closerie des Lilas was one of Hemingway's favourite places to drink and write.
LEFT: In the ring at a local gymnasium.
OPPOSITE ABOVE: Climbing the stairs to Hemingway's first apartment.
OPPOSITE BELOW: Cézanne, another great influence on Hemingway's writing.

LEFT & BELOW: Hemingway, wounded by a falling skylight, left Paris in 1928 but returned to 'the city I love best in all the world' when it was liberated from the Germans in 1944.

ABOVE & OPPOSITE ABOVE: Fifty-five years later, I storm up to the Arc de Triomphe in a Second World War American tank.

OPPOSITE BELOW: After being stopped by the gendarmes, unable to start again. Film crew try the impossible, push-starting a tank.

SPAIN

RIGHT: The calm before the storm. Pause for reflection at the Hotel La Perla, with bulls who've already run their course.
OPPOSITE: Bulls enter the Calle Estafeta, as I watch from the balcony of the room used by Hemingway in the 1920s.

ABOVE: The Pamplona squeeze. Huge, soggy crowd cheers the start of an eight-day party.
LEFT: A bull gets his man.
OVERLEAF BELOW: Apprentice plays bull as I learn, far too late in life, to wield the *muleta* and strut like a matador.
OVERLEAF TOP: In Madrid, football supporters don't care too much about the Hemingway connection.

TOP: Valencia's *Fallas* Festival. Papier mâché model of Spielberg looms over the Titanic and assorted Oscars.
CENTRE LEFT & RIGHT: Fallas processions.
RIGHT: Bullfighter Vicente Barrera is a trained lawyer and as clean-cut as a choirboy. Difficult to square his appearance with the fact that he kills over two hundred bulls a year.

TOP & LEFT: Every day at two o'clock a crowd engulfs Valencia's main square to be blasted by the mighty explosive event they call *Mascletá*.
CENTRE: At the *corrida* (the bullfight) in Valencia. Vicente Barrera, bedecked in *traje de luces*, his suit of lights, completes a pass.

TOP: All that's left of a year's painstaking design and construction.
ABOVE & LEFT: King of the *Fallas* – a fifty-foot-high model of Gulliver is the last of the city's effigies to be torched.
OVERLEAF: Surreal moment. Gulliver has gone, but some of his companions have missed the flames.

mous. A sign hangs above a ground floor doorway announcing the presence of 'Agence de Voyages – Under Hemingway's' (Under Hemingway's Travel Agency). There is a plaque on the wall marking Hemingway's presence here, though it was not put up until 1994, thirty-three years after his death.

We're admitted by a stout old concierge with wispy hair, a floral apron and a tired old dog. She says her parents knew the Hemingways, and produces a photo. Then she indicates a steep corkscrew of a staircase, on which we, like Ernest and Hadley before us, toil up to the third floor.

The Hemingway apartment is once again occupied by an American in his twenties. John, a Bostonian who works for the business consultancy firm Arthur Andersen, is friendly, if a little weary of welcoming devotees. He says that around a dozen people ring the doorbell every week and the Tokyo Broadcasting System has beaten us to it by three days.

He lets us come in and look around the tiny area which, thanks to tongue and groove boarding on the walls and Artex cement work on the ceiling, has absolutely no semblance of period atmosphere. I do get quite excited when he tells me it's up for sale, though I have to remind myself that it is no more than a room, oblong and quite cramped, with a tiny kitchen and a tiny bathroom.

The only real indication of the presence of Hemingway is in the asking price. One million francs. Or £100,000, or 150,000 euros or $180,000.

The look of the surrounding neighbourhood which Hemingway brings to life in such scabrous detail in the first chapter of *A Moveable Feast* cannot have changed that much. The buildings have aged a little – they seem to be tipped back at a slant to the street, leaning towards each other at odd angles as if tired of standing upright, but they are the same buildings. Around the corner in rue Descartes there still stands the one-time hotel where a wall-plaque says Verlaine died and in which Hemingway took a garret room to write.

Looking a little closer I can see that there are changes of detail. Where the goats were milked, there are car-parking spaces to let for $150 a month, and the Café des Amateurs, which Hemingway lovingly recalled as 'the cesspool of the rue Mouffetard', is now a decorous café full of students and tourists.

The rue Mouffetard itself is still cobbled and it follows a narrow, sinuous course down the hill from the Place Contrescarpe. This morning it is filled with a food market of such abundance that filming amongst the aromas of roasted almonds, crêpes, coffee, fresh-baked bread, cheeses, hams, herbs, and fresh-cooked chickens is exquisite torture. The difference is that the fresh food on the street is no longer cheap and those Hemingway would have called the real Parisians are crowded into the supermarket on the corner.

Turn along by the river to the Place Saint-Michel where Hemingway sat in a café and drank Rum St James, 'smooth as a kitten's chin'. He recollects finishing a story here, which made him feel 'empty and both sad and happy, as though I had made love', after which he ordered a dozen oysters and a half-carafe of dry white wine to celebrate.

Today the square is full of an odd mixture of policemen and people in white lab coats chanting and bearing placards. I'm told it's a mass protest by dentists.

Walking on, I pass L'Escorailles, the brasserie which used to be the famous Michaud's, in whose toilets Scott Fitzgerald had shown Hemingway his penis, seeking reassurance because Zelda, his wife, had told him it was too small. No plaque on the wall to this effect, I notice.

Content myself with peering in the window as Hemingway and Hadley did the night they saw James Joyce and his family in there, tucking in, all speaking Italian.

Thirsty by now, I fetch up at an intimate little spot on the rue de l'Odéon by the name of the Dix Bar. The intimate peacefulness doesn't last long as a group of enormous French rugby football supporters, well oiled by jugs of *sangría*, start belting out songs, as the French do at the drop of a hat. This reminds me that next to food, drink, writing and making love, Hemingway liked Paris most for its sports, both as participant and spectator.

Get talking to a young American called Brian who, lured to Paris by the enduring Hemingway myth, gave up his job producing a TV chat show for NBC to become a writer. He's been here a couple of months and so far Paris has exceeded his expectations. Art and aesthetics are acceptable terms here – not an afterthought, but a first thought, as he puts it. I agree. Where else in the world would you find a café marking its bills 'rendezvous de l'élite intellectuelle' as does the Deux Magots, or a country which, in the nineteen thirties, issued a special postage stamp in aid of The Unemployed Intellectuals Relief Fund.

'You can do just about anything in Paris you can do elsewhere,' he enthuses, 'but somehow things tend to be more interesting here.'

We decide there must be a guided tour exploring the physical side of Hemingway's Paris in what one biographer described as 'the sport-crazy Twenties'. Brian agrees to make a few enquiries and work out a sort of Hemingwayathon later in the week.

On the way out of the Dix Bar, run slap bang into another ghost of Ernest. The shop next door, which sells cheap Chinese imports, was once Shakespeare and Company, a bookstore and library which became a regular hang-out for Hemingway. It was run by an American called Sylvia Beach, one of the very few people he never fell out with. 'She had pretty legs and she was kind, cheerful and interested, and loved to make jokes and gossip. No one that I ever knew was nicer to me.'

Though neither Sylvia Beach nor the original Shakespeare and Company are still going, a bookshop bearing the same name and run on affectionately eccentric lines by an American called George Whitman, has been open for business down by the Seine since 1964.

There has grown up quite a fashion lately for bookstores to provide ancillary services such as food and drink and reading rooms, but George, a handsome man of mature years with a tweed jacket and a mop of chalk-white hair, is way ahead of the game. Shakespeare and Company is the only bookstore I know where you can sleep overnight, be brought a cup of tea in a bed set in an alcove in the middle of the Children's Book department and have Notre Dame cathedral as the view out of your window. The shop is open every day of the year, including Christmas Day, and if you turn up on any Sunday George and his interns will serve you tea.

George welcomes me this morning and apologises for not being a great Hemingway fan. He thinks *The Sun Also Rises* his best book by far, but reckons he was not a patch on Theodore Dreiser.

Apparently Hemingway's behaviour when he visited the old shop was not always the best. When he idly picked up a magazine and found a critical review of his work headlined 'The Dumb Ox', he grew so angry that he punched a vase of tulips, smashing the vase, decapitating the flowers and sending water pouring over the book display – thus neatly endorsing the title of the review. He was also, says George, very bad at returning library books.

'Mind you, Henry Miller was worse.'

We climb up a precarious ladder to George's office on the first floor, passing so many shelves, so densely packed, that it seems as if the shop may actually be held together by its books. It's conceivable that if you remove one strategically placed volume, you might bring the lot down and vanish for ever beneath an avalanche of literature.

For George Whitman this would doubtless be the perfect way to go. George's life is lived around, in, among and on top of books. Pausing only to show me how to turn the light on by pressing a Wittgenstein biography on a shelf beside the door, he shows me into his office. Of course it looks quite unlike any conventional office. It's lined with books, open books are spread three deep on what might be a desk, if you could see it for books, the walls are covered with posters about books, and there is a bed in which he sleeps when his flat above is occupied by a visiting author.

We talk a little about Paris in the twenties and why it was such an attraction for people like Hemingway. George ticks off the reasons crisply. Prohibition, book-burning and a general repressive attitude to the arts in the United States after the war, and of course, a favourable exchange rate which meant Americans could live quite well on very little. And the traditional qualities of Paris: tolerance for the arts, an audience for the avant-garde, an indulgence of experiment. The scale of the city, big enough to encompass cosmopolitan groups, ideas and influences, small enough to be walkable, and intimate enough for people to keep in touch easily. George believes the ferment of ideas that followed the end of the First World War has died down. The city is no longer the artistic focal point it was then. It has different priorities now. Most of the young Americans have business degrees. But he has a regular turnover of would-be writers, helping around the shop in return for as many books as they can read and, if they're lucky, a bed in an alcove in the Children's Book department.

Wake up, heart thumping and very anxious. Vivid dream that I had lost all the film crew's baggage somewhere in the Alps. Could have been prompted by last night's reading of the story of Hadley Hemingway who, early in 1923, lost almost every one of her husband's original manuscripts, at the Gare de Lyon, on her way to join him in Switzerland.

I think I might have had a glimpse of how she felt.

It's Chinese New Year today and at breakfast we toast Basil with coffee and croissants. He says it's the Year of the Rabbit. Must remember to ask him under which animal Hemingway was born.

Today the plans so lightly entered upon over a *sangría* in the Dix bar are set to materialise. Brian, my Hemingway for the nineties, meets me in the Tuileries Gardens for a brisk run to start the day. Jogging through this spectacular park seems a wretchedly trivial activity, dwarfed as we are by magnificent gilded arches, monumental fountains and the massive grandeur of the Louvre.

The only disadvantage of being surrounded by such sumptuous display is that it takes your eye off the dog shit. This is plentiful, and avoiding it demands considerable agility, which probably adds an extra aerobic twist to the exercise.

We run on, past elaborate neo-classical statues which have an odd Hemingwayesque touch to them – elephants struggling with rhinos, lions devouring peacocks – and rest briefly before taking to bicycles near the Eiffel Tower. Hemingway became a devoted fan of French long-distance cycle races and an avid reader of the sport's most influential organ – *Le Pédale*. After this an almost relaxing game of table tennis on a concrete public table beside the Canal Saint-Martin, until we are thrown off by some very small children, followed by proper tennis in the Jardin du Luxembourg, where Hemingway often played, though not, according to Hadley, with great patience.

'Whenever he missed a shot he would just sizzle.' His racket, she went on, 'would slash to the ground and everyone would stand still and cower'.

Brian has not yet run out of sports. In fact he seems to have invented a new one for me. It's a US import called Ultimate Frisbee and, unlikely as it may seem, it's played in the most magnificent of settings – in front of the Hôtel des Invalides, the hugely imposing, gold-domed home for veterans of Louis XIV's wars. When we get there the patch of grass on which they play has been turned into a scene reminiscent of a more modern war, with the participants wallowing in a sea of mud from which a grimy blackened object occasionally emerges and sails through the air.

There look to be about ten participants per team, though it's quite hard to tell where the ground ends and a person begins. With wholly regrettable generosity one of the players comes off to enable me to play. I'm told that the aim is to move the frisbee up your opponent's end and score a goal, but if you receive the frisbee you must stay still until you've delivered it. All this is academic as I spend most of my time just trying to stand up, whilst younger, fitter, infinitely dirtier people slither past me. It's all taken with a seriousness of which Hemingway would surely have approved, though he might have been surprised to find that, once the layers of Parisian sub-soil are removed, at least half these sturdy competitors are women.

Best of all, Hemingway liked to box. He brought a pair of boxing gloves in his trunk with him to France and had barely unpacked before he was challenging Lewis Galantière, a man of exquisite manners who was helping them find accommodation, to a fight in his hotel room. Hemingway smashed his glasses.

Not long afterwards, ever on the look-out for a potential opponent, Hemingway taught his new friend, the poet Ezra Pound, to box. He 'has the general grace of the crayfish', he wrote to Sherwood Anderson.

I have only boxed twice in my life, and both occasions were in the same school tournament. Having disposed of someone as inexperienced as myself in a messy first round scrap, I found myself catapulted into the final to face the only other competitor in my weight, a Junior Schools champion. He was a compassionate man who hit me so hard early on that the rest of the bout felt like having a tooth out under local anaesthetic.

So it is with mixed feelings that I find myself at a ninety-year-old iron-framed gymnasium off the Avenue Jean Jaurès for the early evening boxing class. This takes place in a room off the main gym, which is presently full of middle-aged ladies with their hands in the air. This is the daily aerobics class for senior citizens and it looks much more suitable for me. But it's too late now for, with a charming smile, the boxing teacher, Monsieur Chiche, begins to squeeze me into a pair of recently vacated, exceedingly sweaty, boxing gloves.

Monsieur Chiche is small and built like a barrel, but he must be in his sixties, and I worry that I might hurt him more than he hurts me. This proves not to be a problem as he is only putting on the gloves before turning me over to his son, who is also small but built like a whippet.

Apart from Monsieur Chiche senior I must be one of the oldest people ever to have climbed into this ring. All around me are young, wiry lads, many of them African, who look lithe and mean as they rain punches at each other.

Young Monsieur Chiche shows me the moves, how to protect the face and when to throw a punch. At first he is complimentary about my deft footwork but, after a few minutes of my Ali shuffle, a certain amount of impatience shows through.

'Hit me! Hit me now!'

I close my eyes and think of Ernest and surprise myself with a few well placed hooks.

'Good!' he exhorts. 'Hit me again!'

This time I obey his orders to the letter. One jab goes through his guard and connects with his head. I stop immediately.

'Sorry!'

He smiles and I feel a bit foolish. With one word I've confirmed why an Englishman can never be a Hemingway.

Eat tonight at the Closerie des Lilas, ten minutes' walk from our hotel, and once Hemingway's favourite Paris café. He came here to write and worked on short stories and what was to become the novel, *The Sun Also Rises*.

Hemingway liked the clientele at the Closerie: 'They were all interested in each other and in their drinks or coffees, or infusions, and in the papers and periodicals which were fastened to rods, and no one was on exhibition.'

He later wrote with some disgust of the treatment of the waiter who was forced by the management to shave off his moustache when the Closerie went up-market. Though Hemingway's name is immortalised on yet another piece of metal, attached to the bar next to the dining-room, I don't think he himself would still be sitting there. Not at today's prices.

On the way back to our hotel we pass 159 Boulevard du Montparnasse, formerly the Hotel Venitia where, four years after his arrival in Paris, Hemingway slept with a woman called Pauline Pfeiffer, whilst his family waited for him in Austria.

And I remember to ask Basil about Hemingway's Chinese birth sign. It was the Year of the Pig.

Eight-thirty in the morning and I'm in an operating theatre at the American Hospital of Paris lying on a hospital trolley, my head bandaged with toilet paper. This is not the result of yesterday's sporting feats, it's an attempted recreation of one of the most bizarre accidents of Hemingway's accident-prone life.

It happened in March 1928. In the previous nine months Hemingway had sustained an anthrax infection in a cut foot, grippe, toothache, haemorrhoids, several ski falls as well as having the pupil of his right eye cut open by the playful finger of his son. On the night of 4 March he had gone to the bathroom at his flat in the rue Férou and pulled what he thought was the lavatory chain only to find it was the cord attached to the skylight above him. The skylight came crashing down, slicing into his head. Two weeks later he wrote to his editor, Maxwell Perkins: 'We stopped the hemmorage [Hemingway's spelling] with thirty thicknesses of toilet paper (a magnificent absorbent which I've now used twice for that purpose).'

Which is why I'm lying here in the American Hospital at Neuilly, where he lay seventy-one years ago before being given nine stitches in the forehead. To Professor Michael Reynolds, one of Hemingway's biographers, this was more than just another injury. Reynolds suggests that when the skylight split Hemingway's head open, the pain and the spilling of blood caused him to relive memories of his wounding in Italy which he had desperately sought to suppress: 'When the pain dulled...he knew exactly what he should be writing ... the story was the war, the wound, the woman.'

Or, as it became, *A Farewell to Arms*. Which, let's face it, is a much better title.

Reynolds' thesis is borne out by a remark Hemingway made years later, to Lillian Ross: 'I can remember feeling so awful about the first war that I couldn't write about it for ten years. The wound combat makes in you, as a writer, is a slow-healing one.'

Within two weeks of the injury which left him with a lipoma, a lump of hardened skin, permanently disfiguring his forehead, Hemingway was writing to Perkins that the new novel 'goes on and goes *wonderfully*'.

As I lie staring up at the doctors and the light and the needle and the anaesthetic mask coming towards me, I can't help thinking that there must have been easier ways of dealing with writer's block.

O nce Hemingway had been in a place where he was happy and had worked well, he regarded it in some sense as his property. So, in August 1944, not long after he'd suffered another mangling car accident in the London black-out, he was back in Paris under contract to *Collier's* magazine to play his part in liberating what he called 'the city I love best in all the world'.

Whilst more conventional Allied troops were busy flushing out the remaining pockets of German resistance, Hemingway and an ill-assorted guerrilla band went on to conduct his own personal liberation of Paris, including the Café de la Paix and the Brasserie Lipp, as well as Sylvia Beach's bookstore and the Ritz Hotel, where the barman asked Hemingway what his men would like and received the answer, 'Fifty martini cocktails!'

In the interests of historical research I have been given a chance to experience my own liberation of Paris. We have permission for me to ride up one of the approach roads to the Arc de Triomphe in a World War Two American tank.

Unfortunately the tank is stuck in rush-hour traffic. A chilly, insidious drizzle has descended, as we look in vain among the Renaults and Peugeots of the commuters for the reassuring sight of a gun barrel. When, an hour later, our tank does arrive, it's smaller than I expected – the sort of tank you might use to do the shopping.

An anxious bespectacled face peers apologetically from one of the forward hatches. This is Patrick, the French owner of the tank, an M8 Greyhound with a stubby 37 mm cannon, made by Ford in 1944. After introductions all round, I climb aboard, inserting myself like a shell into a mortar barrel at the hatch next to Patrick. Choosing our moment, we make a slow but spectacular pull-out into the traffic.

Unlike 1944, our progress is almost completely ignored. Though tourists wave and point, the first French people to acknowledge a tank in their traffic are two gendarmes who bring us to an undignified halt half-way up the Avenue Hoche and demand to see our papers.

The good news is that the papers are in order. The bad news is that the tank won't start again. Patrick and his assistant tinker around for a while before diagnosing a failure in the fuel supply. It might take an hour or two to get it fixed, so they suggest we try and kick start it. Just how easily the filming process can turn human beings into automatons is that we all without question agree to Patrick's suggestion that we push the tank.

In 1944 he would doubtless have had thousands of willing volunteers, but today there's half a dozen of us and we manage to shift it only as far as an old lady crossing the road, who shrieks at us in a most un-liberated way.

Patrick notices a tow-truck about to hitch itself to a trailer full of builder's rubble. He races through the traffic and manages to persuade the driver to hook up to the tank instead. He agrees with remarkably good grace and after a moment the

M8's engine is conjured into life with a puff of smoke and a flash from the rear exhaust.

The liberation of Paris is never quite the same after this, but trundling across the cobbles towards the Arc de Triomphe, encased in inch-thick steel, is not a bad way to remember the place.

All that's missing are the martinis.

As we prepare to leave Paris I have the same feelings I always have when I leave Paris. I have been happy here and I'm full of admiration for this well-run city and the way it respects and displays its heritage of antiquity, elegance and culture. But Paris is impossible to thank. It will not soften and allow itself to be hugged around the shoulder as you say goodbye. Unlike Venice, or Chicago, or even New York, it has no sentimental side. It outlasts and outshines everyone, and Hemingway recognised this too.

'Paris', he wrote in a piece for *Esquire* magazine in early 1934, 'was a fine place to be quite young in and it is a necessary part of a man's education ... But she is like a mistress who does not grow old and she has other lovers now.'

By that time there was another place Hemingway had fallen in love with. It was, along with Italy and France, the third, and most important of that triumvirate of European countries in which he felt truly happy. Gertrude Stein had pointed him in its direction and he had already used it as a setting for the novel that had made him famous. It was Spain and the Spanish way of life that were to remain the greatest influence on him from now on.

SPAIN

*In December 1921 the **Leopoldina**, en route from New York to Le Havre, put in at Vigo in the province of Galicia on the north-west coast of Spain.*

'You ought to see the Spanish coast,' Hemingway wrote to Sherwood Anderson. 'Big brown mountains looking like tired dinosaurs.'

And in a letter to his childhood friend Bill Smith, he compared Galicia with north Michigan. 'We're going back there. Trout streams in the mts. Tuna in the bay. Green water to swim in and sandy beaches ... Cognac is 4 pesetas a litre.'

*Though he was only there four hours, he came up with an article on tuna fishing for the **Toronto Star Weekly**. In it, apart from an uncanny foretaste of a later book, is the essence of all that attracted him to Spain.*

'The Spanish boatmen will take you out to fish for them for a dollar a day ... It is a back-sickening, sinew straining, man-sized job ... but if you land

a big tuna after a six-hour fight, fight him man against fish when your muscles are nauseated with the unceasing strain, and finally bring him up alongside the boat, green-blue and silver in the lazy ocean, you will be purified ...'

Struggle, peasant pride, redemption through physical pain, the confrontation with nature that strips away sham and compromise. This is what comfortable, bourgeois Oak Park Ernest saw in Spain and it drew him like a magnet.

Pamplona, capital of the proud and ancient Spanish province of Navarre, is a sturdy walled town girdled with modern housing blocks and the gleaming factories and assembly plants that are the rewards of belonging to a greater Europe.

Its name is known all over the world for the running of bulls through its streets at the festival of San Fermín. Though there are seventy such bull-runs all over Spain, this is the one everybody knows about. That's because Ernest Hemingway came here.

So I can't help thinking about him with mixed feelings as I arrive late on a cool afternoon, with a light drizzle falling on me as I push my way through an army of Hemingway-driven celebrants back-packing their way into town.

Pamplona is preparing to receive this army. Barriers are going up on the roads, and prices are going up in the bars. Few will have booked far enough ahead to find a room. Most search out doorways, park benches, traffic roundabouts or simply sleep where they fall. Hemingway's part in establishing the international reputation of the fiesta is celebrated by a series of red wall-posters showing his venerable bearded likeness, which are attached to any building with which he was connected.

There is one on the wall of the hotel in which I have a room – the Hotel La Perla, tucked away in a corner of the big central square, the Plaza del Castillo. The Hotel Quintana, which was cheaper and where Hemingway preferred to stay, is no longer in existence.

La Perla manages to be discreet and at the centre of the action at the same time. Inside it exudes an old-fashioned respectability. The lobby gives on to a dimly lit salon filled with long-case clocks, gilt-framed mirrors, crystal chandeliers and two stunningly incongruous bulls' heads thrust lugubriously out of one wall on either side of a portrait of the bullfighter Lalo Moreno, brother of the hotel owner. He looks grave, as matadors tend to do.

When Ernest and Hadley first discovered the fiesta, they reckoned they were the only English-speaking people in town. Nowadays you can barely find a table outside La Perla that is not occupied by a hard core of world-wide fiesta addicts who return here every year. There is a strong Swedish contingent. One of them, Hans Tovoté, known to everyone as 'To-To', has written a novel about Pamplona, and another, Alf Tönnesson, has booked room 217, the one Hemingway stayed in, until the year 2040. There are Norwegian, French and British groups, with their own clubs and insignia. There are numerous bearded Americans who look like Hemingway and many more pretending to *be* Hemingway.

I walk through the arcades of the square to the Café Iruña, which displays another Hemingway poster. He and his friends would hang around here watching the action and drinking absinthe (now considered too strong to be legally served). It features heavily in *The Sun Also Rises* and, with the help of a jug or two of *sangría*, you can slip quite effortlessly back into the Lady Duff Twysden era. Only when you look more closely at the passing crowd, do you realise that time has moved on.

A procession approaches, demonstrating for the release of ETA (Basque Nationalist) prisoners, still held for terrorist activities. Then they in turn are gone, swamped by the crowd of lanky, baseball-hatted international youth slowly taking over the Plaza before the big day.

I catch sight of a copy of *El Mundo*. It has a page devoted to San Fermín on the Internet. The headline reads 'Gracias a Hemingway'.

'At noon of Sunday July 6th the festival exploded, there is no other way to describe it.' Hemingway's description in *The Sun Also Rises* (published as *Fiesta* in Europe), captures the moment but hardly does justice to the build up.

The streets at the heart of the city are cordoned off to all but essential traffic – drink deliveries, street-sweepers, ambulances – as we join the tide of humanity flowing inexorably down cobbled streets with boarded-up windows, towards the Town Hall where the opening ceremony takes place.

The correct outfit for San Fermín is a white shirt, white trousers and a splash of red – a neckerchief, a sash – in memory of the blood spilt by the saint himself when he was beheaded, or, some say, killed by bulls, over a thousand years ago.

What seems to be absolutely obligatory is that you drink as much as possible and what you don't drink you spray all over your friends. So bottles of *cava*, Spanish sparkling wine, are popular, as is a cheaper alternative called *kalimotxo*, a mixture of wine and Coca-Cola made to a simple recipe – buy a litre bottle of Coke, drink half and fill it up with wine.

From our camera position at a third-floor window we watch a group of young men and women, some in green plastic hospital gowns, rush into the square carrying a bucketful of booze, two large bags of flour and a stack of egg boxes. Now I know why half the balconies are shrouded in plastic sheeting. Within minutes flour and eggs are flying from all sides.

With half an hour still to go before midday, the crowd is glued together in one single, sticky mass, a pulsating human pancake, dancing, shouting and chanting on a carpet of slime and broken glass. A boy with short, spiky, peroxide blond hair leaps onto one of the columns on the town hall façade and, thrusting out his chest like a modern-day St Sebastian, screams at the crowd to throw things at him. Bottles of *cava* are shaken furiously and released in a thousand mini-orgasms as the crowd hysteria builds towards the one great unifying climax of the midday rocket.

It sounds like hell, but it is a hell of exuberance – a manic, but largely good-natured, yell of liberation. I'm just noting down this *bon mot* when there is a crack on the glass, followed by a roar of approval as a second egg whistles in, scoring a direct hit on our sound man.

At a minute or two before twelve, those cameras not disabled by edible missiles can send their viewers throughout Spain and the rest of the world pictures of the town officials, in braided frock coats and old-fashioned tricorn hats, stepping out on to the ornate Town Hall balcony to an immense reception.

'San Fermín! San Fermín!'

Trumpeters step forward and blow a fanfare which no one can hear, after which, accompanied by one last cataclysmic bellow, the midday rocket goes up and eight and a half days of non-stop partying begins.

Below us the mass of people squeezed near to suffocation point begins to shift and break up as it spills out of the square and into the surrounding streets, which are full of sodden, egg- and flour-encrusted groups imploring those on the balconies above to tip buckets of water over them.

Up one side street is a drinking fountain with a central tower about fifteen feet high. This has been colonised by young Australians and New Zealanders who dare each other to climb up and throw themselves off. The only safety net between them and the pavement is the crowd itself.

By the time we get back to La Perla the Plaza del Castillo has been transformed. Young, unsteady people of all nations are swaying about. A flopped-out figure wakens to find his friends have tied his hands to the bench he's been sleeping on. High-pressure water jets scour the space around the bandstand sending an arc of plastic and glass bottles scudding across the ground towards the circling garbage trucks.

I talk to two regular American visitors. Curly is tall with a stack of grey hair; his friend, who introduces himself, without irony, as John Macho, is short and stocky. As the rubbish swirls by behind them they declare themselves Pamplona addicts. They love the fiesta, the people, the bulls.

Most of them know somebody who has been hurt in the bull-run and Curly has had his leg broken. His injury, as with most others, was not caused by a bull but by someone trying to get out of the way of the bulls. A fifty-something man from Austin, Texas, offers me several reasons why this will be his fifth consecutive year on the bull-run, of which the most intriguing is: 'It's an aphrodisiac, Michael. Believe me.'

Believe him or not, I can't help thinking Viagra would be a lot easier.

Whoever you speak to, the talk is all of the next high – the *encierro* (running of the bulls) which will begin tomorrow morning at eight o'clock sharp.

There is not much rest to be had in Pamplona tonight. Those who have run with the bulls before will try to sleep as best they can. Those who haven't will, likely as not, have been awake most of the night saucing themselves up. Those of us who are here to film have to be getting into positions on the course by six o'clock. And the noise goes on. It's like the night before battle.

Stepping out of La Perla into that half-day, half-night just after the dawn breaks is like stepping into a time vacuum. All the people who were on the square last night are still there, wearing the same clothes. The same music is playing from the same bars. The same street-cleaners are cleaning the same patches of street. Only the smell is different. Fortified by the excesses of the night, the town radiates a sweet, sickly smell of stale booze. An indoor smell that's been let out. The soles of my shoes stick to the flagstones of the arcade. The religious and the bacchanalian seem to merge seamlessly at the festival of San Fermín.

The *encierro* is the name given to the driving of the bulls from their corral on the outskirts of town to the ring in which they will fight later in the day. Over the years it became a feature of the Pamplona *encierro* that locals and visitors would try and run before the bulls along a course of just over half a mile. The event was in full swing before Hemingway whetted the world's appetite by describing it in his first bestseller, *The Sun Also Rises*. Later, James Michener helped things along with his book, *The Drifters*.

With endorsements from authors like Hemingway and Michener, running with the bulls became one of the great international tests of maleness, a chance to participate in an ancient tribal rite, still surviving in the midst of modern Europe. More recently, women have been allowed to run. Whether this will eventually deal the macho tradition a mortal blow remains to be seen.

Not that I can see many women on the streets this chilly morning. The participants are almost exclusively male and range from the experts, mostly Spanish, who take it seriously and will remain as close to the bulls as possible, to the young, already drunk college kids for whom this is just another stop on the dangerous sports circuit.

I have been invited by Alf and To-To, the two Swedish *aficionados*, to watch the run from the balcony of the room Hemingway took at La Perla. This gives directly on to the narrow street called Calle Estafeta. Before they reach here the bulls will have run uphill from the corral into the Town Hall square, left at Chargui Ladies Lingerie, past Liverpool Video Club and Compact Disc Centre and sharp right at Ana's jewellery shop. There are no barriers in this street, and nowhere to hide, so man (and woman) and bull will get pretty close to each other.

With an hour still to go the balconies are filling up with families, friends, and those who've rented these viewpoints for thousands of pesetas. At 7.30 police and colourful officials in scarlet berets and tunics begin to clear the course. Anyone poking out of a doorway is pushed firmly back in. At 7.40 a squad of street-cleaners comes through, personal high-pressure vacuum cleaners strapped to their backs, followed by a second line with brushes and black rubber buckets. At 7.45 the live television coverage begins and I can see our street on a screen in the building opposite. With ten minutes still to go, an eerie, unnatural calm descends. The runners, held in groups at different starting points, shift from foot to foot, lick their lips and tighten their grip on the rolled-up newspapers which are traditionally carried with the hope of landing a thwack on a passing bull.

At 7.52 a safety announcement is made in different languages. At 7.55 I catch a glimpse on television of one of the bulls, still in the corral, steam rising gently from his nostrils, his great head framed against the green hills beyond the city. Nothing in the four years of his life so far can have prepared him for what is about to happen.

At eight on the dot the rocket goes off, the bulls are released and all the concentrated energy that has been building up to this moment crackles along the course, a psychic shock-wave that affects the most dispassionate spectator. When the bulls come in sight they seem the calmest creatures in town, running in disciplined order behind accompanying steers, heads lowered, eyes forward, whilst humans scamper hysterically around them flicking their papers and occasionally grabbing at a horn.

In a few seconds they've gone past, and everyone looks to the nearest television screen to see what really happened. I see one brown bull run close to a barrier, stripping off its line of spectators one by one. They're already playing back a goring which took place outside Ana's Jewellers. Then the second rocket sounds, indicating safe arrival of the bulls at the ring.

To-To consults his watch.

'Two minutes thirty seconds. That's good.' He seems vaguely disappointed.

'The longest I ever saw lasted fourteen minutes. One bull was detached from the rest and then they turn angry, you know. There was quite a pile-up.'

The runners filter back into the square and soon the bars and cafés are full of tales of daring exploits and valiant feats with rolled-up newspapers.

Rumours of serious injury, even death, chase round the city. One positive fact, reported in the *Diario de Navarra*, is that thirty tons of broken glass were removed from the streets yesterday.

On Hemingway's advice I leave the hotel at half past five this second morning to be sure of a ringside seat to watch the amateur bullfight that takes place at the end of the *encierro*. 'Pamplona is the toughest bullfight town in the world,' he wrote in the *Toronto Star Weekly*. The amateur fight that comes immediately after the bulls have entered the pens proves that.'

This may be Ernest pumping himself up a little for, though there is no evidence that he ever ran with the bulls, there is a photograph of him dodging horns at the 'amateurs'.

Certainly the ring fills up fast, but the great number of spectators are teenagers, excited boys and girls who throw themselves energetically into Mexican waves and sing-alongs. A tired brass band plays in the middle of the ring. The only really hard behaviour comes from an angry young man with a shaved head who seems determined to take on the rest of the world with a virtuoso display of taunts, leers and obscene gestures.

The crowd takes against him immediately. He is punched and kicked and pushed down the stands into the ring where, to enormous applause, the police lead him off. Support for the authorities seems unanimous.

Eight o'clock comes round and we hear the rocket that means the bulls are on their way. Only seconds later the first wave of runners spills into the ring, jogging briskly. They are followed by a second wave running more smartly, who are in turn followed by a third wave sprinting like hell. Almost unnoticed in the middle of all the human hysteria are the bulls, trotting in resolutely, rarely breaking their stride as they follow their guiding steers across the ring and away into the pens where they will stay until they go out to be killed nine hours later.

This leaves the ring full of several hundred amateurs. A couple of American boys from Arizona who I'd met earlier in the day have run for the second time. Their eyes are shining as they shout at me from the other side of the barrier.

'It was incredible.'

'Frightening?'

'Terrifying! But we did it! We did it!'

'Now you're used to it will you become a regular?'

'No way! No way!'

At that moment a gate swings open and they leap to safety over the barrier. They needn't have worried. The animal that is released for the amateurs to try their skills on is not a bull, but a thin, though sprightly, cow with the points of its horns taped. It frisks off amongst the crowd, picking off people here and there. The crowd is very fair, any attempt to grapple the cow to the ground or even pull its tail being roundly booed.

After a while the cow is brought back in and there is a brief pause before the next one emerges, which gives a chance for the bolder boys to play chicken by sitting in the ring as close to the gate as possible. Those brave enough to remain at the front can scarcely avoid being trampled by the animal as it's released.

This mass larking about goes on for another half-hour, and by nine o'clock the bullring starts emptying and the streets start filling again. Outside, by the television mobile trucks, a line of Hemingway fans waits to be photographed at the bust of Ernest which stands under the trees of an avenue called Paseo Hemingway. His head and shoulders seem trapped in the bulky granite plinth as if he's half stuck in a recycling bin.

The celebrations seem to have mellowed out on this second day. The dangerous sports boys have either crashed out on distant camp-sites or left town, looking for the next adrenalin rush. There are more locals on the streets, more bands playing, more families, more dancing and more entertainments laid on by the infinitely patient authorities of Pamplona. The police, who once fought the crowds here, seem to have learned the lesson that a crowd is only really dangerous when it has an enemy.

At La Perla a woman in a dressing-gown, smoking and agitated, is in the lobby trying to make the receptionist understand that her hand-bag has been stolen from her room. She went down the passage to the lavatory and when she came back it was gone. A moment later it's found. In her room. There's a lot of this hyperactivity around but I've seen little crime and almost no aggression. But the pace is relentless and

there is a sense in the air, if not of self-destruction, then something pretty close to it.

It certainly stimulated Hemingway's imagination and his
third visit here, with his Anglo-American friends in July 1925,
provided him with personal intrigues worthy of the location.
By the time he left for Madrid he was putting the place and
the people together in his mind, and when he reached Valencia, a fortnight later, he was ready to write the novel that
immortalised Pamplona.

Seventy-four years later, I'm leaving too. From the train
window the sharp-ridged mountains and the twisting green
valleys of Navarre are broadening into the plains as I head
south to see Madrid and Valencia for myself.

Hemingway was always more intrigued by bullfighting
than bull-running. He was fascinated by matadors, whom
he described memorably in *Death in the Afternoon* (1932) as
'affable, generous, courteous and well liked by all who are superior to them in station, and miserly slave drivers with those who
must work for them'.

When he first visited Madrid in 1923 he was still starry-eyed
and chose to stay at the Pensión Aguilar in Via San Jerónimo
'where the bullfighters live'.

We are quartered in the Hotel Suecia where the Hemingways took a suite on his last visit to Spain thirty-six years later.
The hotel does not seem to know, or care, that he stayed here,
which is quite refreshing in a way, if a little odd, as the cultural
centre next door is running an exhibition called 'Hemingway y
España', consisting mainly of photographs of Ernest on that
trip in 1959.

The pictures are quite sad. His powerful build is much
reduced and the white beard and wispy white hair make him

look more like some venerable old prophet than a man only just out of his fifties.

A first visitor to Madrid could do worse than follow the Hemingway trail, not just because so much of it still exists, but because he was a man of taste and did not waste his time on the second-rate.

Across the road from the hotel is the Prado, one of the world's greatest collection of paintings, where Hemingway caught up with his beloved Bruegels and Goyas and where I could spend an entire visit in front of Hieronymus Bosch's *Garden Of Earthly Delights*.

Then follow him, for refreshment, into the old quarter west of the Prado, where the narrow streets bear the names of writers like Cervantes and Lope de Vega and take a beer at the Cervecería Alemana, a 96-year-old bierkeller with Spanish tiling and an open unfussy interior, which was one of Hemingway's favourites. (If you feel oppressed by the presence of the Great Man, I recommend La Venencia just round the corner in the Calle Echegaray, of which there is no record of him ever entering. The speciality is sherry served from the cask and the peeling walls are stained a rich tobacco brown.)

Hemingway would likely have repaired at this point for a cocktail in the Art Deco elegance of Chicote on the Gran Vía, a cocktail bar founded in 1931 'to promote talk and opinion'. Chicote earned Hemingway's undying loyalty by never closing throughout the bombardments of the Spanish Civil War. There's another photo of him here, from 1959, frail and bearded.

Though you may be hungry by now, remember that Spanish restaurants don't expect you for dinner until well after nine. Hemingway fans will take his recommendation and head straight for Casa Botín, which has been serving meals for over 200 years and whose wood-fired ovens turn out herds of roast suckling pig every night. It's easy to find. Down the steps at the south-west corner of the Plaza Mayor, into Calle Cuchilleros (Knife-maker Street) and it's practically next door to a restaurant with a large sign, 'Hemingway Never Ate Here'.

As it is inconceivable that anyone but an invalid should be in bed in Madrid before one-thirty, I'm easily tempted into a post-prandial night-cap. We head for the focal point of the old city, the wide cobbled expanse of the seventeenth-century Plaza Mayor with, at its centre, a fine statue of Philip III on a charger. The Plaza is grand, but car-free and friendly and full of bars which make it almost impossible to cross without feeling thirsty.

Bar Andalú, like Botín, is traditional, but 'traditional' in Spain is not so much of a tourist board cliché as it is elsewhere, and generally means something still very close to the spirit of the country.

Three great bulls' heads loom out of the wall surrounded by an exhaustive collection of framed photographs showing matadors in moments of cape-swirling glory or gory and gruesome injury.

Machismo drips from its tiled and trophied walls, and it is perhaps no coincidence that, as I eventually leave to totter home, I notice for the first time the truly heroic proportions of the testicles on Philip III's horse.

Hemingway, Spain and bullfighting are inseparable. After his visit in 1923 in which he wanted to live where the bullfighters lived, he was, as you might say, hooked.

He returned year after year. The bullfighter first appears in his books in *The Sun Also Rises* and, a few years later, in an exhaustive *aficionado*'s guide called *Death in the Afternoon*, which James Michener called a kind of Bible of bullfighting.

It still is one of the best books on this arcane art.

Hemingway returned to the subject in 1959, when he criss-crossed the country to chronicle the series of *mano a mano* (one-to-one) contests between two leading matadors. *Life* magazine had commissioned a 10,000-word piece, but he turned in a first draft of 120,000 words, reduced to 45,000 after his death, and published in 1985 as *The Dangerous Summer*.

Whatever I feel about bullfighting, I can't come to Spain and avoid it. I decide to follow the advice Hemingway gives in the opening chapter of *Death in the Afternoon*.

If those who read this decide with disgust that it is written by someone who lacks their ... fineness of feeling I can only plead that this may be true. But whoever reads this can truly make such a judgement when he, or she, has seen the things that are spoken of and knows truly what their reactions to them would be.

So here goes.

Thirty minutes south of Madrid, in flat hot countryside, is a farm where bulls are bred for the ring. It is owned by José Antonio Hernández Tabernilla, a lawyer whose family has bred them since 1882. He has records that trace the ancestry of each bull as far back as 1905.

José Antonio and his wife are a tall, handsome couple, courteous, well informed and much more comfortable with English than I am with Spanish.

The farm is functional, with low outbuildings and nothing fancy other than a barn in which are displayed old stirrups, halters, bridles, saddles and various other taurine and equestrian accessories. Framed bullfight posters hang on the walls, of which the most curious is one detailing a *corrida* (the Spanish word for a bullfight) specially laid on for Heinrich Himmler in 1940.

Apparently the famous Nazi found the whole thing too

cruel and left after the second fight.

They introduce us to a stocky man in early middle-age who wears a T-shirt and a white straw hat with 'Benidorm' on the ribbon. This is Serafín, the farm manager. He is shrewd, and taciturn. More comfortable with bulls than the BBC. We are piled unceremoniously into a farm trailer, and with Serafín driving the tractor, and two or three dogs running on ahead, we're hauled along a bumpy track into the fields where a hundred and forty Santa Coloma fighting bulls are kept. Most of them appear to be sitting comfortably in a pear orchard at the far end of a wide paddock. They like the shade there, says José Antonio, and they love the pears.

José Antonio explains that they mustn't have too much contact with humans, as this may compromise their fighting ability later. In fact the calmer and quieter a state they can be kept in the better.

There is a sudden commotion at one end of this taurine health farm as two of the ash-grey bulls spar up to one another. Instantly the dogs race off and separate them. Which is quite something to see. These are two- and three-year-old bulls and look quite big enough to me, but by the time they have reached the fighting age of four they will weigh between 500 and 600 kilos – over 1200 lbs.

Serafín examines each bull with a critical eye, the strength of their shoulders, the size of their horns, already singling out those that will make the best fighters. José Antonio says that though he's proud of rearing good fighters, Serafín 'suffers terribly to see his animals die.'

José Antonio feels bullfighting has changed. Like everything else it is adapting to the market, to the needs of television. He used to send his bulls to Pamplona, but they don't want them any more because their horns don't look big enough.

Back at the farm, refreshment is provided. The irresistible *jamón serrano* (cured ham), olives and wine. I practise drinking the farmers' way – from the spout straight into the mouth, or in my case, down the shirt.

On our way back to Madrid, near the town of Arganda, we stop at a triple-span bridge over the River Jarama. A big new road is being put through here and in amongst the rubble and the electricity pylons is a ten-foot-high metal star, leaning at an angle, surrounded by weeds. A plaque beside it marks it as a monument to the International Brigade, those volunteers from outside Spain who came over to fight against Franco and Fascism in the war of 1936–9.

The Spanish Civil War, the second of three wars in which Hemingway saw action, and the one which produced his novel *For Whom the Bell Tolls*, was the most politically committed time of his life. He wrote commentary and helped raise finance for a propaganda film, shot by a Dutchman, Joris Ivens, and called *Spanish Earth*.

Orson Welles, enlisted to record the commentary, wanted to change some of the lines which he thought sounded unduly pompous. At a viewing of the film, described by Welles in *Cahiers du Cinéma*, he and Hemingway came to blows, going at each other with chairs and fists, as the armies fought it out on the screen in front of them.

The two American heavyweights were reconciled over a bottle of whisky, and though Welles still gets the credit in some of the early prints, it is Hemingway's flat, harsh monotone that accompanies the film.

It's half past eight on a Sunday morning and in the hard dry sunlight a group of prostitutes is working a corner of the Casa de Campo, one of the great straggling parks of Madrid.

Not that that's why I'm there, though my business in the park at this time is essentially macho. In amongst the prostitutes and the pine trees is an Escuela de Tauromaquia, a school of bullfighting.

Yesterday I witnessed the care and attention that goes into raising bulls to be killed. Today I am to witness the equal amount of care and attention that goes into killing them.

The school, considered the best in the country, has its own miniature ring and whitewashed outbuildings, on which are painted the breeders' marks, which will be found branded on every bull. They are sometimes letters, sometimes symbols and have an ancient cabalistic feel to them.

Inside the ring the class is assembling. All boys (though there is one potential female matador), mostly in their teens with the quick eyes and lean, combative stance of lads from the streets. But appearances can be deceptive, and one eighteen-year-old, Fabian, turns out to be from a Mexican family who had enough money to send him to school in Texas in the hope of curing his desire to become a bullfighter.

That didn't work and he has not only been attending classes here for three years, he has also dispatched fifteen or sixteen bulls already. He shrugs off my incredulity. One of the top three bullfighters in Spain, El Juli, is only seventeen years old, he says, and smaller than him.

A portly older man enters the ring and calls the boys together. They address him as *maestro* and I assume that one day before his stomach grew he was as light and lithe as the boys he's teaching. He picks up two *banderillas*, the spiked sticks which are placed in between the bull's shoulder blades as it charges, and begins to demonstrate the moves.

The bull is, I'm relieved to see, not flesh and blood, but a set of horns and a padded cushion fixed to a bicycle wheel. One boy races this contraption fast across the ring and another has to go close enough to drop the barbed prongs exactly parallel to each other in precisely the right spot. Nine out of ten times they fail, but, as Fabian points out, only one or two of this class of thirty might be good enough to even contemplate fighting professionally.

Under Fabian's guidance I am allowed to try some moves with the cape, pink on one side and gold on the other, with which the matador tries to tire the bull in the second stage of a fight. The first thing that strikes me is how heavy it is, heavy enough, of course, to maintain its shape in all weather conditions.

Fabian corrects my posture, emphasising the importance of the strut, of thrusting the hips forward, of staring the bull down. I ask him what he thinks when he's confronted with the bull. Does he have to hate it?

'No, no,' he shakes his head firmly. 'The bull is my friend.'

I'm rather touched by this, until he adds, 'He makes me look good and make a lot of money.'

How much money?

Fabian considers for a moment. The top fighters? Around $80,000 for a *corrida*, in which he will fight two bulls. From that he will have to pay his team – his *picadors* and his *banderilleros* – but if he fights fifty times in a season his earnings are into the millions. And then there's advertising, public appearances, opening supermarkets.

I look around me. A big clear sun beats down on the ring. Half the apprentices are practising their passes with the cape and half are clutching horns and racing at them. I'm struck by how absurd and how deadly serious it is at the same time.

In the dedication required bullfighting has overtones of medieval knights and chivalric orders, of ancient rules and disciplines. Of something almost monastic.

I thank Fabian and wish him well. I suppose a time will

come when he will be hurt, does that worry him?

'Oh, yes.' He nods and smiles, 'Oh, yes.'

I must say, understanding bullfighters requires dedication too. Now I have to find somewhere in Spain where I can see them in action.

Atocha Station in Madrid is a rather wonderful combination of ancient and modern, achieved by building a completely new terminal without pulling down the old one.

The platforms are laid out beneath a superstructure of concrete columns, functional and practical and quite severe, while the old nineteenth-century station, cleaned and restored, now houses a tropical garden around which are seats and cafés, from which you can look up at the incongruous cloud of steam drifting from the jungle up to the roof.

We climb aboard a train for Valencia, following in the footsteps of Ernest and Hadley who left Madrid for Valencia in 1925 on their way back from Pamplona.

Hemingway knew there was a story to be written about what had gone on in Pamplona that year, but was torn between his need to write it and his need to see as many bullfights as possible. Valencia, where there was a midsummer *feria* (a festival with bullfights), seemed the ideal combination. Work in the morning and the *corrida* in the afternoon. And it worked. *The Sun Also Rises* was begun in Valencia in July 1925.

We head south-east towards the Mediterranean leaving behind the huge housing blocks of Madrid's new suburbs and crossing the dry, parched plain of La Mancha. It stretches wide and flat and almost treeless to the horizon, marked by the outline of a range of mountains that never seems to get any closer. An occasional farm, drifting smoke, a gypsum plant, a grain store, a line of white-washed windmills, a castle on a hill, everything seems detached, distant, as if reluctant to be on this great exposed plain at all.

After three hours the line cuts down through the edge of the plateau and in amongst the mass of orange groves from which Valencia has made its money.

Valencia Norte is the loveliest, least rugged, least bombastic of stations. The way out takes you through a turn-of-the-century Art Nouveau concourse, across a brown and white chequered marble floor, beneath a ceiling of coffered wood and walls of multicoloured mosaic tiles to a low white exterior, decorated with stucco oranges and orange leaves.

The next thing I notice is a huge frankfurter driving by, passing a twenty-foot-high brightly coloured statue of a bare-breasted lady, and a long line of women and children in eighteenth-century costume walking behind a vigorous, if discordant band.

We have arrived at the time of year when Valencia goes crazy. The festival of *Fallas*. The time when, we are told ominously, nobody sleeps.

I'm woken by a series of sharp explosions in the street below. A salvo of fire crackers. Then another, then another. There is a moment's calm and my eyes are gently closing when, with a short warning squeal, a pipe and drum band starts up below the window.

Downstairs on the way to breakfast I ask the hotel receptionist what is going on. She tells me, brightly, that the noise and the music are the work of *les despertas*, the waker-uppers, whose job it is to go round the city rousing those who might have defied all the odds and fallen asleep during the night.

'They want you to go and see their *fallas*,' she explains.

She hands me a brochure called 'Living *las Fallas*', which

she says will help me enjoy the festival. A quirkily translated introduction advises the visitor to 'leave your prejudices and timid fears behind' and to 'accept human ridicule in an absurd world'.

Venturing out to accept ridicule I find a city out on the streets and not taking itself at all seriously. Crowds amble around inspecting the various colourful, rude, sexy, satirical papier mâché effigies they call *fallas*, which are erected in squares and on street corners throughout the city by various neighbourhood groups. There are apparently seven hundred of these sculptures all over Valencia, and all will be set alight at midnight on the feast of San José, which is the day after tomorrow.

The origins of *Fallas* lie in the middle of the eighteenth century when the local carpenters would burn all their winter shavings, off-cuts and general rubbish in one big fire which they would sometimes decorate with a makeshift figure of some kind.

They're a lot more complex and sophisticated nowadays, but the intention remains to poke fun, to be disrespectful and entertaining at the same time.

Hard by a handsome eighteenth-century church in the Plaza del Pilar rises a huge and curvaceous flapper girl surrounded by a grotesquely made-up Mae West stretched out on a couch, alongside beaded madames and crazed sax-players. Outside the central market is a looming likeness of Steven Spielberg aboard the *Titanic*, holding a film camera from which springs the *ET* bicycle.

Politics, the church and the media are popular targets for the designers. At one *falla* I notice a real life TV presenter being filmed in front of a grotesque and joyfully lewd carica-ture of a trouserless television presenter.

Just as I'm feeling rather thankful for my anonymity, a short fair-haired man hurrying by turns and stops and greets me cordially. He says we've met before, at one of Graham Chapman's parties in the early seventies.

His name is Robert Misik and he's a Dutchman living and working in Valencia. He offers his help if there's anything we want. There is, of course. Like tickets to one of the bullfights and a bullfighter who will agree to talk to us.

Robert barely blinks at this and, after a quick exchange of numbers, vanishes into the crowds who are now gathering two or three deep along the route of yet another procession. This one lasts several hours as women from the various *falla* groups carry flowers through the city to a forty-foot high wooden effigy of the Virgin Mary. Every offering of flowers is then handed up to a special team which arranges them into a giant floral-tapestry. It sounds awful but it is done with great style and as it seems to give at least half the entire female population of Valencia the chance to participate, it is also truly democratic.

This evening, over a very fine meal of crayfish and delicately cooked, zingily fresh *merluza* (which sounds so much more exotic than hake), Robert brings us the good news that one of the top matadors at this year's *feria* has agreed to meet me early tomorrow morning, the day before his fight.

Vicente Barrera, grandson of Vicente Barrera the matador whom Hemingway takes to task for his killing technique in *Death in the Afternoon*, is, it goes without saying, slim and good-looking. These seem obligatory qualities for a bullfighter.

He's also thirty years old, a couple of months older than my eldest son, which is considered, in his profession, to be getting on a bit. Everything about him is neat and restrained, from his taste for plain expensive clothes in autumnal colours to the formal but immaculate cut of his jet-black hair. He looks like a choirboy.

We meet in a very ordinary *mesón*, a local bar with tiled walls and hams hanging from the ceiling.

There is a bit of a hiatus as our director, always a stickler for veracity, had been assured that *criadillas fritas* – fried bull's testicles – are a speciality of the *mesón*, and wants me to nibble one or two on camera as we talk. It turns out that, like the Monty Python cheese shop, they have lots of them normally but today the van broke down. Robert is out combing Valencia for fresh testicles.

Whilst we wait, Vicente, in a soft voice and with continual apologies for his English, tells me about his background. He only took up bullfighting six or seven years ago, and like Fabian in Madrid, against his father's wishes. He had trained as a lawyer, though he adds, with a self-deprecating laugh, that it was lucky for all clients that he never practised. He is now among the top ten fighters in the country, appearing at something like a hundred *corridas* a year, in Spain, France and across the Atlantic, in Mexico, Peru, Ecuador, Venezuela and Colombia.

Robert arrives, breathless, holding a paper bag. There are no bull's testicles to be found so he has bought pig's instead. The director approves and they are sent to the kitchen to be prepared, reappearing quite soon, sliced and fried and ready for the interview.

I ask Vicente why he became a bullfighter.

'Next to being Pope, it's the only thing,' he smiles, but it isn't entirely a joke.

'It is the most important thing I can do with my life.'

'There are many people who think that bullfighting is cruel.'

He turns aside a moment and when he turns back his politely courteous manner has slipped a bit.

'What do people in an office in ...' He searches for a name, '... in New York, know about bulls? *We* know about them. *We* live with them.'

He points at a piece of cooked meat on display by the bar.

'This animal ... what is this animal?'

'Cow?'

'Cow, yes, a cow. A cow has six months. A bull has four years, living wild in the country.' He turns again to the cooked cow. 'Who is this animal? You don't know. We know the father, the mother of the bull, we put the name of each one on the bull.'

Vicente is undergoing an almost Clark Kent-ish transformation as he warms to the theme.

Bullfighting, he says defiantly, is something that cannot be done without passion. Technique is nothing without passion. He grabs at his cashmere sweater as if wanting to tear out the heart beating beneath it and show me the passion inside.

'You live your passion all of the day, you know. You don't have holidays, you don't have weekends, you don't have family, you only have your passion and the *toro* and the fiesta and no more.'

'Do you still have fear?'

He looks at me pityingly.

'Of course! If they don't have fear, they are crazy people! Matador is a person I think normally very intelligent and normal. A brave person is not someone who has no fear!'

I am not sure if this vehemence is the frustration of a highly educated, sensitive man continually forced to defend something at which he is particularly gifted or just a demonstration of the pride and controlled aggression which makes him able to do what he does.

All I know is that I would never describe anyone who stares a charging bull in the face two hundred times a year as normal.

But this is exactly how Vicente seems when the interview's over. He returns to his soft-spoken, almost solemn politeness, shaking all our hands and inviting us to come and see him fight tomorrow, and to go backstage afterwards.

Whereupon he slides gracefully out into the street leaving me alone with a plate of pig's testicles, by now greasy, congealed and ready for my close-ups.

This morning the pipe band and its attendant explosions passes, with scrupulous punctuality, at ten minutes past eight. This time I don't take it lying down. I stagger to the window and peer through the curtain.

I suppose I had expected to see young children following the band like a Pied Piper, ebulliently scattering fireworks. In fact, the procession consists almost entirely of elderly men, one of whom pushes a supermarket trolley brimful of firecrackers which his two lugubrious companions light with their cigars and toss across the street.

This is the last day of *Fallas*, the culmination of a week's festivities. Tonight, at midnight, the statues all over the city will be torched, though the largest one in the main square will not go up until an hour later. Vicente's bullfight begins at five, so we ask the ever-enterprising Robert how we can best kill the time. He suggests more noise.

At two o'clock every afternoon during the festival there is an event known as the *mascletá* in which the three big pyrotechnic families of Valencia vie with each other to produce the most powerful explosive display, and as today is the last day of the last festival of the century, and the millennium, Robert reckons it will be one of the best.

He calls some friends who have an apartment over the square and they invite us to watch the performance from their balcony.

It is a perfect day, bright, cloudless with a dry, fresh breeze. An hour before the display is due to begin, the Plaza del Ayuntamiento is already impassable. The crowd, estimated at two to three hundred thousand, is kept behind barriers allowing access for the Red Cross emergency teams who occasionally dive in to retrieve someone overcome by the crush. In the centre of the square the men from the fireworks company work quietly away, checking the network of wires from which hang thousands of small packages of explosive, and loading up rows of mortars.

Our kind host José Luís Soler, an architect, offers us a drink and a piece of sliced sausage and advises us to keep our mouths open during the display as it takes the strain off the eardrums. And don't use earplugs, let the blast through.

Three shells fired high into the air signal the start of the onslaught. The fuses are ignited, releasing a thunderous wall of sound which rolls towards us, the speed of the explosions carefully orchestrated to vary the pace whilst building up a counterpoint of overlapping echoes. One huge report follows another, the blasts hurling shock-waves across the square, strong enough to send my jacket flapping. The pace accelerates as the fire sprints along the wires of thunderflashes, sending up a ripping, shattering din, and when you think you can take no more, the big mortars start to blow with such force that you can only hang on and let it thrill and terrify. A final, ferocious amalgamation of sound, fed by thunderous explosions on the ground and soaring shell-bursts in the air, builds to a relentless, ear-splitting cacophony, an unbelievably tremendous roar, which, with one last mighty salvo, stops as suddenly as it began. Which was, according to my watch, five minutes and eight seconds ago.

For a fragment of time complete silence falls, then with a great cry, the crowd spills through the barriers and races across to the fence to salute the pyrotechnic team, who emerge like mythological heroes from the shroud of white smoke they have created.

Ticket-touts are out at Valencia's graceful brick bullring long before this afternoon's fight begins and the souvenir-stalls are doing brisk business selling scarves, packs of cards, baseball hats, T-shirts and key-rings bearing likenesses of the stars of the circuit, though I notice a range of car-window ornaments offers Jesus and General Franco as well.

I hire my cushion and search out my seat on the bank of long concrete terraces. There is a mix-up however and the seat is already taken. Then, just as I'm desperate, fame comes to the rescue. No sooner am I identified as the killer of small dogs in *A Fish Called Wanda* than I cease to be a troublemaker and am treated most cordially by all. The man whose seat it is introduces himself as Paco and orders his wife and friends to squeeze up and make room for me.

Paco, in a smart grey lightweight suit, looks like a late-middle-aged businessman. Like his wife and friends, he seems to be dressed more for the opera than the bullring.

Each of the three matadors fights two of the six bulls, and Vicente's first bull is the third of the afternoon, indicated as weighing 600 kilos and hurtling into the ring like a tank on steroids. Vicente, in black hat, blue and gold suit of lights and pink stockings, mops his brow with a towel before going forward.

The most unpleasant face of bullfighting, in which the bull is drawn away to charge a heavily armoured horse (whose vocal cords have been cut to prevent it whinnying) takes longer than usual and the crowd don't like it.

Vicente draws the bull away with his cape and fights close and is generally thought to have done well.

The fifth bull is fought very stylishly and the matador, Enrique Ponce, has the crowd on its feet in appreciation. He is awarded two ears by the judges, an acknowledgement of great skills.

This is a hard act to follow, and as the sun moves off the stadium and a brisk night chill comes on, Vicente appears to be coping well. The music plays a *paso doble* for him, as it does when particularly artistic moves are executed, but when it comes to the kill, things go wrong. This is the most dangerous moment for the bullfighter, for, although his bull is weak, he must at this point take his eyes off it and hope to bend himself and his killing sword over the still lethal horns to deliver the *coup de grâce*. Vicente has to take three serious risks before he can dispatch the bull. The crowd is unappreciative.

When Robert and I get to Vicente's minibus after the fight, the atmosphere is not good. Vicente is angry with his *cuadrilla* – his support team in the ring – for not preparing the last bull properly. In between tearing them off a strip he has to switch on a flashing smile for the fans thronging the van.

When eventually we manoeuvre our way through the crowds and reach the hotel, there are more adoring fans waiting for photographs, autographs and handshakes. He deals with it all very patiently and delivers grave, long-suffering smiles.

Back in his room his real feelings surface. He is angry at the way things went and is clearly regretting his promise of an interview.

He disappears to the bathroom, leaving us with his valet, a small dark gnome-like older man with very black hair and thick eyebrows who is given to much shaking of the head and muttering. Robert whispers to me.

'He's saying this is very irregular.'

Vicente reappears. There is still no sign of our crew. He smiles thinly and stands beside a small table on which I notice pictures of the saints and the Virgin. I don't like to ask right now, but Robert tells me later that it is a portable chapel, laid out by his dresser so that Vicente can pray before the fight. All bullfighters pray before a fight.

Vicente is completely preoccupied. His hands and body keep repeating the movements of a pass rather as a golfer might replay a putt that let him down.

A mobile phone rings. He looks up. It's our film crew, calling to say their vehicle is stuck in traffic. Human traffic. The doorbell goes. A woman from Spanish television regards us anxiously. Did we know that Vicente had promised to appear on a live discussion programme in ten minutes' time?

Vicente's dresser shuts the door on her.

Vicente looks forlorn, well as forlorn as a bullfighter in a bejewelled suit worth $3000 can look. His face betrays the strain of a profession caught between the demands of ancient tradition and modern exploitation. As we shake hands he apologises. This weekend there is a lot of pressure on him. He is fighting again tomorrow and the night after in Alicante.

'I'm playing with my life each night,' he says, almost bitterly. And in his case it is probably true.

Five minutes to midnight in a small square in the heart of the old city. There isn't room for that many people and those that are here are mainly local. They're gathered around a tall, Disneyesque Aladdin, centrepiece of an Arabian Nights fantasy with prominent local politicians, nuns, and a bishop or two thrown in for good measure. It's an elaborate and clever piece of work and those who created it are now busy making sure that they can destroy it just as cleverly. They move around the base of the figure poking an air-hole through here, laying a fuse there. One man is up a ladder at the back of the statue, sticking wires and paraffin bags up Aladdin's backside.

The mood is serious and celebratory at the same time. I have the feeling that the general success of *Fallas* is considered more important than any single event. The groups compete with each other but only to make the whole festival better. Which is why this festival has been marked by high spirits without violence, drinking without fighting, noise without aggression. And tonight is perhaps the most precarious balancing act of all. Seven hundred bonfires are about to be lit across an urban area of a million people.

At midnight in our quiet square the local queen of the *Fallas* lights the fuse that starts the last act of this extraordinary festival. Lines of firecrackers and flame race towards Aladdin's buttocks and other strategic flashpoints. For a while the figures prove resistant but gradually the flames take hold and the figures are stripped to their wooden frames and for a half-minute or more the surge of the fire is frighteningly intense.

We make our way towards the main square. Over the heads of the crowd by the market I can see Steven Spielberg's glasses melting. At the end of one street fire licks round a Harlequin, at another, a Roman Emperor and several naked ladies are engulfed in flames.

It takes most of one hour to make our way the short distance to the main square. A figure of Gulliver fifty feet high towers over us and is duly ignited (this time via a main fuse which runs straight into his fly). As the final conflagration takes hold Gulliver's head collapses, sending his rather soppy Hollywood-style grin crashing on to the street. The *bomberos* (firemen) spray the nearby palm trees as the flames leap and the heat intensifies and once again we hold our breath not knowing which way it will go.

Two-thirty in the morning on the streets of Valencia. The bulldozers and trucks are moving into the main square to remove the remains of Gulliver.

The brushes are revolving on a squadron of natty little cleaning vehicles. A line of orange-clad street-sweepers, with gleaming new brooms and shovels, stands ready to follow them.

Though the celebrations still go on, the party's over. A sense of loss hangs in the smoke-shrouded air, a muted feeling of anti-climax, a sudden acknowledgement that the city of Valencia is dog-tired.

I know I shall miss being woken by *les despertas*, I shall miss being able to stroll round Spain's third biggest city as if it were my own living-room, and when in the morning I hear the noise of a city returning to normal – the car alarms, the police sirens – I shall probably miss the explosions too.

There is something intoxicating and dangerous and reckless in the way the Spanish celebrate, which is what must have drawn Hemingway to their way of life. It is physical and hard and colourful and noisy and yet has a rare sense of historical continuity.

Throughout his adult life, with the exception of the darkest years of General Franco's dictatorship, Hemingway kept coming back to Spain. In a drawer in the house in Ketchum, where he shot himself on 2 July 1961, were tickets to the Pamplona bullfights that were to begin a week later.

KEY WEST

In the late nineteen twenties a gently rising tide of fame was beginning to lap around Ernest Hemingway and he was not altogether happy about it. Paris had changed. There were too many tourists pointing him out on the street. Too many tourists in Paris, period.

He had a new wife, Pauline Pfeiffer, and he wanted to come home, but to somewhere where he would not be bothered. His friend, the writer John Dos Passos, recommended Key West, the southernmost city of the USA. No more cold European winters, a tolerant, relaxed atmosphere and plenty of deep-sea fishing. On top of all this, Pauline's rich Uncle Gus lived not far off, in Arkansas. When Ernest and the second Mrs Hemingway arrived in Key West he promised to have a brand new car waiting for them. A generous gift, but not absolutely essential. In 1928 there was no road connecting Key West with the rest of America. As Hemingway wrote to Dos Passos in February 1929: '45 mile water gap still and the County Treasurer absconded with all funds and they've closed the schools – let alone build the road.'

Once he'd got used to the heat, Hemingway became wildly enthusiastic about Key West. He sent out a flurry of letters to tempt his friends to visit him in what he called 'the St Tropez of the poor'. He told his editor, Max Perkins, that he had salvaged fourteen bottles of Château Margaux from a wreck on the reef, that the shooting and fishing were fantastic and he had some pre-war absinthe he wanted him to try. He told Dos Passos he was absolutely broke but in one evening had seen 100 tarpon (a large gamefish), and was already planning to take him out fishing to the Tortugas.

Hemingway was good at persuading people that they wanted to do things he wanted to do, and a crowd of his buddies soon descended on the sleepy city. They came and went on the railroad that was built in 1912 and remained the only land route through the Keys until it was destroyed by a hurricane in 1935.

Hemingway was greatly affected by the hurricane, one of the worst in living memory, with winds of 250 miles an hour. He was furious that the weather service had down-played it so much that a camp of war veterans working on the new highway was not evacuated and hundreds were drowned. In a letter to Max Perkins, he was especially incensed about a writer who had come to the Keys because he needed a hurricane for the book he was writing:

Max, you can't imagine it, two women, naked, tossed up into trees by the water, swollen and stinking, their breasts as big as balloons, flies between their legs. Then, by figuring, you locate where it is and recognise them as the two very nice girls who ran a sandwich place and filling station three miles from the ferry ... I would like to have had that little literary bastard who wanted his hurricane along to rub his nose in some of it.

Today, as I drive south on US One from Miami, it's hurricane season again. I'm on Seven Mile Bridge, the longest of the connections between the islands, with the Gulf of Mexico on one side and the Atlantic on the other, washing in over the long coral reef, six miles out. The sea is peaceful in all directions, the heat intense.

Remains of the shattered railway, which, as Hemingway accurately predicted, was never rebuilt after the hurricane, can still be seen: chunky stone towers marooned in the shallow water.

Despite the splendours of this bridge, much of US One is a two-lane road with the feeling of going nowhere in particular. Driving through sedge-grass and mangrove swamp, passing straw-thatched pull-ins offering tropical cocktails, and signs warning of crocodiles crossing, I feel as if I've broken free from the corporate compounds of urban America and entered an unreal world where illicit pleasure is permitted and irresponsibility actively encouraged.

Of course it's an illusion. Corporate America has its grip on the Keys like anywhere else. There are condos and apartment hotels and expensive resorts owned by insurance companies. It's just that the grip seems a little looser here, and the feeling grows the nearer you get to Key West.

Not for nothing is US One known as the Overseas Highway. By the time I'm driving its last mile, past the clapboard colonial villas of Whitehead Street and the wide-open doors of the Green Parrot – 'Last Bar on US One' – it is not the Keys, but the rest of America that has become remote and unreal.

*

Ernest Hemingway would have been a hundred years old today and I can find no mention of this fact in the newspaper. I check the date again, July 21st 1999. But there's nothing there. My copy of USA Today is still full of news of the death of JFK Junior in an air-crash at the weekend. The grief of the Kennedys has eclipsed the celebrations of the Hemingways.

But he is not forgotten here in Key West. Indeed every year at this time, in the height of sub-tropical summer, men with beards don thick woollen sweaters in imitation of their hero and gather in the steamy heat of a downtown bar to see who looks most like him.

The Hemingway Look-Alike Contest is one of many highlights in a ten-day orgy of Ernestness called the Hemingway Days Festival, which also features competitions for storytelling and arm-wrestling. Flicking through my programme I see that the centenary will not go unnoticed. A giant birthday cake will be cut outside Sloppy Joe's Bar at six.

Sloppy Joe is a potent figure in Hemingway mythology. His full name was Joseph Russell; a native of Key West, married with three children, he had first endeared himself to Hemingway by cashing a thousand-dollar royalty cheque from *A Farewell to Arms* which the First National Bank had refused to do on account of Hemingway's scruffy appearance.

Hemingway liked a drink or two and though the sale of alcohol had been illegal in the States since 1920, Joe Russell ran a speakeasy and a 34-foot ocean-going launch with which he brought liquor in from Cuba, only ninety miles to the south. Hemingway joined him on some of these trips, slaking his considerable thirst and gaining, besides an appetite for marlin-fishing and Havana night-life, the basis for a character in one of his novels. Joe Russell, rechristened Harry Morgan, became the anti-hero of Hemingway's Gulf Stream novel, *To Have and Have Not.*

When Prohibition was repealed at the end of 1933, Russell opened a new, smarter Sloppy Joe's on the premises of a bar called the Blind Pig. This is where, in December 1936, Hemingway first encountered the good looks and powerful personality of a young novelist and reporter by the name of Martha Gellhorn, for whom he ditched Pauline three years later.

In May 1937, after a quarrel over rent, Sloppy Joe's moved to where it is now, on the corner of Greene and Duval Streets. It's here in the last, and for him, the least-visited of the three Sloppy Joe's, that the Hemingway flame burns brightest, and tonight its unremarkable two-storey brick and plaster façade is garlanded with red and blue ribbon and, at intervals along the top of the building, are long white birthday candles and the message 'Happy 100th Birthday Papa'.

In the street outside, a crowd has gathered around an immense cake, probably twenty feet in circumference, its icing gently fermenting in the evening sun.

No one can be suffering more from the effects of Key West's devouring, energy-sapping humidity than a Scottish pipe band which suddenly appears, dressed head to knee in black and squeezing and puffing out a bagpipe version of 'Happy Birthday', their faces leaking like boats in a storm. At the end of this a great cheer goes up and on the roof, two men, bandanna-ed like a pair of hippie terrorists, fire off shells which scatter confetti over the throng. All of which seems to have about as much to do with Hemingway as the Hemingway key-rings, frisbees, golf-balls and yo-yos that can be acquired at Sloppy Joe's gift store.

The commercialisation of Hemingway is not a new phenomenon, nor was it something he actively discouraged. In the early 1950s he gave his name and, one presumes, his creative talent, to an ad for Ballantine Ale. 'I would rather have a bottle of Ballantine Ale than any other drink after fighting a really big fish,' he enthused.

Even in Key West he was already aware of his celebrity potential. In a joky piece written for *Esquire* in 1935, he told readers:

The house at present occupied by your correspondent is listed as number eighteen in a compilation of the forty-eight things for a tourist to see in Key West ... between Johnson's Tropical Grove (number 17) and Lighthouse and Aviaries (number 19).

To discourage visitors while he is at work your correspondent has hired an aged negro ... who meets visitors at the gate and says, 'I'se Mr. Hemingway and I'se crazy about you.'

Today his house has moved up to the top of the charts and visitors are met at the gate with a charge of $7.50 for adults and $4.50 for children and a sign reading 'Do Not Pick Up Cats'. The cats are, to be honest, a bigger attraction than Hemingway. There are over sixty of them strolling, sleeping, washing and occasionally leaping about the house and grounds in proprietorial fashion. They are reputedly descended from Hemingway's six-toed cats and the sure sign of this is that half of them are still polydactyl – that is, they have a bit to spare in the toe department. Some have six, others seven or even eight. They lighten up what is otherwise a pretty lifeless series of rooms, and they give the guides something to talk about.

'This red one here is a marmalade tom we call Bill Clinton. He has seven toes, and yes, he *has* been neutered.'

All the rooms are fully accessible except for his writing room, located above one of the outbuildings. It was once attached to the rest of the house by a rope bridge, which must have tested Papa's sobriety. It is unconvincingly pristine, with dead animals on the wall and the obligatory typewriter as its central feature.

(Hemingway seems to have had as many typewriters as he had cats.) Visitors peer into this sanctum from behind a screen of Spanish-style wrought-iron bars, as if about to see someone tortured on the rack.

By the end of the tour I feel sorry for Pauline, Hemingway's second wife, who, with the help of Uncle Gus, created this home for him. Our guide holds her responsible for the fact that we are all dripping with sweat. According to him it was Pauline who apparently removed the ceiling fans and had them replaced by elaborate wood and glass chandeliers.

'And *she* was fashion editor of *Vogue*!' Gentle titter.

'Maybe it was a different *Vogue*.' Bigger, if slightly uncertain, titter.

At the side of the house, next to the gift shop, is a murky green swimming pool. Our guide indicates a penny coin, sealed in the limestone paving beside it, and tells the story of how Pauline had the pool built in 1937 for the then substantial sum of $20,000. When Hemingway heard the price he was so disgusted he said something to the effect that as she had spent everything but his last penny, she might as well have that too, whereupon he'd flung down the coin we see today.

There is no mention of the fact that Hemingway had been away two-timing her with Martha Gellhorn in Madrid and that the pool had been paid for, like so many other extras in Key West, by generous Uncle Gus. But then, this is the Ernest Hemingway House, not the Pauline Hemingway house.

Hot, and a little bit bothered by all this, I cross the road to Ernest's Café for a large 'smoothie', a big, refreshing pick-you-up of crushed fruit and ice. The bearded and bespectacled face of the great man growls down at me from T-shirts which the management is not allowed to sell owing to a copyright dispute with the house across the road.

From what I've read about Hemingway, he was very demanding of his friends, expecting loyalty and constant availability. His omnipresence in Key West makes him almost impossible to avoid and I feel myself suffering a severe attack of Hemingway-induced claustrophobia – as if I might find some manifestation of him in my bedroom cupboard or sitting next to me at dinner.

To clear my head I walk west down Whitehead Street, and find myself in a Hemingway-free zone of gracious, well-restored nineteenth-century timber and clapboard houses, many of which bear plaques indicating that they were built by wreckers and spongers. Ships regularly went aground on the coral reef and the opportunist seamen of Key West made a considerable living from salvaging the wrecks. That's when they weren't sponging, I mean, sponge-fishing.

Number 305 Whitehead is a pretty, balconied and balustraded building called '"Wrecker" Johnson's House', built entirely from the wood of submerged ships. Further down is the finest house on the street, the Geiger or Audubon house, saved from demolition in 1958 and now immaculately restored to its neoclassical glory with wide, shady balconies to catch the breeze, and inside a considerable number of bits and pieces, like a fine set of Chinese porcelain, that never made it past the reef.

Key West is that rare thing in the USA, a truly walkable city. The streets are mostly tree-lined and shady and in a short distance you can ring the changes from tourists and bars on Duval Street, to quiet backstreets with soothing names like Angela and Petronia. The trouble is that Key West is on the same latitude as Mecca and it can get very hot.

Which is why I end up talking to the local mayor, Wilhemina Harvey, at the end of the day, when the temperature is down to the low 90s and we can see the town from an air-conditioned car. Mayor Harvey has ruled Monroe County (which includes Key West and beyond) with charm, humour and, doubtless, a rod of iron, since 1980. She's eighty-seven and not planning to retire. She's a social liberal, very popular with the gay community, she tells me. As this comprises over a third of Key West's 25,000 permanent residents, she should be there well into the next millennium.

We talk of all sorts of things, from the current sewage pipe leaks which have forced Key West's beaches to close and for which she has applied for Federal Aid, to the separatist tendencies of this part of America. People born and bred in the Keys are called Conchs (pronounced 'Conks') after the sizeable local shellfish. There is a Conch Republic, with its headquarters in Key West and its own flag.

Mayor Harvey tells a good tale of meeting the Queen when she visited the Keys recently and presenting her with a conch shell which Her Majesty gratefully accepted. Only afterwards did the Mayor remember that she had not had time to warn her that conchs bring bad luck if taken indoors. She and her friends had a good laugh about this, until, a week or so later, Windsor Castle's library burned down.

I feel obliged to mention Hemingway, thinking that she, like me, will be happy to avoid the subject for a while. Quite the opposite. She has fond memories of him coming in to her family drugstore.

'He was a quiet, almost shy man till you got to know him.'

Try telling that to the Hemingway look-alikes.

Somewhat reluctantly plugging myself back into the world of Key West's best-loved son, I search out the Hemingway suite at La Concha Hotel, which, at six storeys high with a tower on top, looks big and bulky amongst the neat, low-rise streets around it. It was opened in 1926 in anticipation of a tourist boom. Instead the Depression came along, Key

West stayed poor and La Concha was spared a rival.

It hasn't changed much and probably should, certainly in the elevator department. A one-legged man with a hod of bricks could have got up to the sixth floor faster than the lift I'm in. Nor is there anything very special about the Hemingway Suite, except for its current occupant.

Kevin is a New York policeman who makes my obsession with Hemingway look like mild interest. He runs with the bulls at Pamplona, has taken the Hemingway Suite at the Sun Valley Lodge and says he once broke down in tears after clearing four feet of snow off Hemingway's grave in Ketchum cemetery.

Though Kevin has a spiky red beard and looks more like my auntie than Ernest Hemingway, it doesn't surprise me that he has entered the look-alike competition, nor that he is through to the finals. Spiritually, Kevin is clearly a contender, and if this were a be-alike competition he'd win horns down.

He's a little uncomfortable about the Suite. A guest recently checked out complaining of hearing someone else in the room and waking up to feel an invisible pressure on the end of the bed. Another guest cut short a booking giving no reason at all. I should imagine that any manifestation of Ernest would be just what Kevin wanted, but for a New York cop he sounds remarkably squeamish about the other side and suggests we continue the conversation in somewhere resolutely corporeal, like Sloppy Joe's. Sloppy's is basically a watering hole. A great crowd of people, including one man wearing a Viking helmet, are clustered round every available inch of bar and table, shouting against the thudding rock music, dealing with beers or simply chewing away on some of the house specialities – 'The Bun Also Rises', 'For Whom the Grill Tolls' or a simple Ernie Burger, 'a giant half-pound burger from the cattle ranches of Key West'.

Ceiling fans stir the fetid air, giving a gentle flutter to the dusty flags that hang down over the bar. A painted marlin arches across one wall, and Hemingway's great rock of a head stares back at me from the black back-cloth behind the band.

Kevin talks fast, his clipped New York delivery jarring amongst the southern drawls of Florida. He brushes aside any questions of what books of Hemingway's he may have read. His is not a literary thing, it's a mind thing.

'I'm a man of action. A romantic activist. I'm a chaser of bulls and a dodger of boredom. Boredom', he says, fixing me with a manic stare, 'is a very, very scary thing.'

From what I've seen, Kevin's fellow contestants look an amiable bunch. Does he detect a generosity of spirit amongst the look-alikes?

'No, they hate me. They can't stand me.' He smiles cheerfully at this and his eyes go slightly misty.

'I've been taking abuse down here for ten years ... and now I'm like a local. Ask anybody, I'm a local legend down here now.'

He has a plan for tomorrow's final. For his presentation he's going to team up with an even more venerable local legend, an 83-year-old by the name of 'Shine' Forbes, who boxed Hemingway back in the thirties. I should come along. This could be Kevin's year.

I accept his invitation to be a sort of unofficial second, but I'd like to meet Mr Forbes for myself.

A local cartoonist called David Laughlin offers to introduce me to Shine. Laughlin is slim and softly spoken, with long hair and a golden beard. He was raised on an Amish farm in Ohio, thinks laid-back Key West is becoming too rich too fast and is contemplating a move to New Zealand. He has a healthily sceptical view of the local life-style and particularly the Hemingway worship. In one of his cartoons a bull sits pounding away at a typewriter beneath a head of Hemingway sticking out of the wall.

Shine Forbes's house on Fort Street feels more Caribbean island than American mainland. This is the cheaper end of town and has a quite different and much more seductive atmosphere than the manicured main drags round Duval Street. It's known as Bahama Village.

Shine sits out in a small patch of yard, drinking a Bud from the neck in the shade of a tree. Chickens scratch and strut in the dust. I've noticed chickens all over Key West, occasionally causing cars and bikes to skid to a halt as they potter across quite busy roads. 'Why do the chickens cross the roads?' I ask Shine. He tells me that many of them are descended from the roosters who were bred for cock-fighting, which, until two years ago, was a common occurrence in Key West, and one of the reasons Hemingway liked the place.

Shine, whose real name is Kermit Forbes, is amused but not greatly impressed by the celebrity that being Hemingway's sparring partner has brought him. He lives modestly in a rented single-storey clapboard house which was once a dairy. Now it's home to Shine's rich collection of memorabilia. There's a pair of boxing gloves with the stuffing spilling out, masks from the Halloween procession, beads, necklaces, a Conch Republic flag, a young child's woollen dress, soft toys, bar mirrors, two teddy bears in a net, a cactus growing from inside a bright yellow kettle. And that's just outside.

Indoors there's barely room for the two of us amongst more mouldering toys, baseball hats, birdcages and photographs of Shine with various friends, which hang from the ceiling as densely packed as leaves in a tropical forest. On one wall is a picture of young Shine, fists raised in fighter's pose. Next to it is Hemingway, his great barrel chest bared, a cloak around his shoulders, beaming broadly as he leans on the ropes of a boxing ring.

One day, some time in the 1930s, Shine was acting as a second to a young boxer who was taking quite a pasting. Shine threw in the towel. The referee refused to accept it. He did it again and once more the referee kicked it away. Furious at his refusal to stop the fight, Shine climbed into the ring and swung a punch at the referee. Only after the fight was Shine told that the referee he had assaulted was the famous writer Ernest Hemingway. He was made to go round to the house and apologise straightaway.

Shine knocked on the door of the grand house at 907 Whitehead with deep misgivings, but Hemingway, far from being angry, asked him and his friends in for some sparring practice and told them to come round any time.

And they did. One Christmas, Shine recalls, they were walking up Whitehead, short of cash, when they saw a light in the Hemingways' house and knocked on the door. Hemingway was holding a party and the boys earned $200 sparring by the pool as an entertainment for his guests.

Shine finishes his Budweiser and sends the bottle skimming across the yard. One of those sparring friends, who went by the name of 'Iron Baby' Roberts, is being buried this morning but Shine doesn't think he'll go along. He doesn't like funerals. And he looks like the sort of man who doesn't do anything he doesn't want to do.

He stares for a while across to the chain-link fence on the other side of the street, which surrounds a now abandoned military base. He flicks a fly away. I ask him if he ever hurt Hemingway. He rubs the flat of his hand across his bad eye and chuckles.

'I could never get near him. He was a big man.' He mimes Hemingway's long arms. 'I had to look up to see him.'

I ask him if Key West has changed a lot since the days when he helped milk a cow in the house he now lives in.

He looks around, never hurrying to answer. 'Sure.' His eyes come back to mine. 'No one's hungry any more.'

As we're leaving, Basil notices a cockerel lying in a corner of the yard. It's been very still for an awfully long time. He brings it to Shine's attention. Apart from confirming that this is an ex-rooster, he doesn't seem much interested.

'What do you do?' Basil enquires solicitously. 'Bury him?'

'We'll bury him.' Shine yawns expansively. 'Or throw him over the fence. He'll go over the fence one day.'

As will we all.

Seven o'clock in the evening outside Sloppy Joe's and Kevin the cop is not a happy man. His chance to win the Hemingway Look-Alike competition at the eleventh attempt is only an hour away and Shine Forbes has not shown up.

'Goddamit, where the hell is he?' mutters Kevin, puffing nervously on his cigar, his eyes flicking over the growing crowd.

Kevin is not the only one of the twenty-four finalists to be displaying uncharacteristic jumpiness (though Hemingway himself once said that the only two things that really frightened him were snakes and public speaking). Most pace quietly up and down, like little boys before a school play. 'Just talk loud and slow,' one contender is counselled. Another sits quietly with his wife and daughter, dressed, like Kevin, in the all-white strip and red neckerchief of a Pamplona bull-runner, every now and then running his tongue over dry lips.

Meanwhile the judges, who are all previous winners, are behaving with the assurance and swagger of those who know they have the destinies of others in their hands. Wearing medal ribbons round their necks, they're photographed and eyed-up and accorded all the guarded respect of school prefects.

Kevin's loyal friend Devin is quite sure that the secret of a Hemingway winner is social. The oligarchy of previous winners who run the Look-Alike Society are searching not for a Hemingway replica but for someone they'll all get on with. According to Devin this counts Kevin out.

'If there were twenty-four contestants, he'd come twenty-fifth.'

When I see his act I'm not really surprised. He skips up on stage to a raucous but generally friendly welcome and, wielding his cigar like George Burns on acid, goes into a suicidal routine, berating Shine – 'that prick' – for not having turned up to fight and roundly abusing every one in sight before ending with the observation that now JFK Junior is dead he, Kevin, is the sexiest man in the USA. The packed crowd boo and hiss him like they might a pantomime villain.

He comes off-stage, wild-eyed, hyped up and delighted.

Most of the other acts confine themselves to anodyne statements of admiration and respect, though I quite like the middle-aged man who does a strip-tease, peeling off his safari shirt to reveal a firm if ample belly over which he proudly rubs his hand. 'A vote for me is a vote for Hemingway in his prime.'

Predictably, Kevin the cop fails to win again. Equally predictably, he is already making plans to come back next year. Devin, doubtless adept by now at consoling his friend, wonders why nearly all the contestants want to look like Hemingway when he shot himself. Which is a fair point. The image of Hemingway sanctioned by the Hemingway Look-Alike Society and Sloppy Joe's Bar, joint organisers of the event, is the bearded, poloneck-sweatered likeness, complete with tired eyes and thinning hair, captured on camera by Karsh of Ottawa four years before his death.

There is no place here for a young, fit Hemingway, a Hemingway who looks like the way Hemingway did when he lived in Key West.

We're about to leave the sauna-like climate here at the end of America. Sixty-six summers ago Hemingway too was planning to escape the sub-tropical summer.

Over a farewell margarita or three made for me by Joan, the barwoman at La Concha, I reflect that what motivated Hemingway to travel, apart from natural curiosity, was a mixture of boredom and boastfulness. Having sought new places and new experiences, he used all his old reporter's wiles to make it seem that he was the first to discover them. So, whether it was ambulance-driving in World War One, or marlin-fishing, or bull-running at Pamplona, Ernest Hemingway had the canny knack of being the first to tell the world about it.

In the sticky heat of July 1933 he was putting final touches to what was to be another world exclusive. And, for him, a new continent.

AFRICA

'I like to shoot a rifle and I like to kill and Africa is where you do that.'

*So wrote Hemingway to Janet Flanner, in April 1933. Hemingway had taken to life in the United States with enthusiasm. He had produced a second bestseller, **A Farewell to Arms; Death in the Afternoon**, an authoritative work on bull-fighting; and a short-story collection, **Winner Take Nothing**.*

*There were rumblings of criticism – Max East-man's review of **Death in the Afternoon** was headed 'Bull in the Afternoon' – but on the whole his reputation was high, and he was enjoying the attentions of Hollywood, which had just made **A Farewell to Arms**, the first picture from his work. Yet none of his plans for 1933, outlined in a letter to Arnold Gingrich, publisher of a new magazine called **Esquire**, seemed to include his native land:*

'I go across to Cuba in a small boat April 12 to fish that coast for two months in case go to Spain

to make a picture, if not, for four months then to Spain. Go from Spain to Tanganyika and then to Abyssinia to shoot. Will be back next January or February.'

His wanderlust had returned. Though he never made the picture in Spain, he did, thanks to a generous loan from Pauline's Uncle Gus, make his first visit to Africa, disembarking at Mombasa, Kenya, on 8 December 1933.

Early January 1999 and I'm standing, drinking my Tusker beer, in an open porch at the front of my tent at the Tortilis camp, on the edge of the Amboseli National Park in south-eastern Kenya.

My guidebook notes that 'Mount Kilimanjaro, at 19,340 feet (5896 metres) the highest mountain in Africa and the highest free-standing mountain in the world, dominates the landscape.'

I can't see it anywhere.

I'm told that you have to be up very early to catch sight of the mountain, as her vast bulk generates an almost impenetrable layer of cloud for much of the day.

To be able, even theoretically, to see the snows of Kilimanjaro less than twelve hours after leaving Europe adds an edge of guilt to my exhilaration. I feel I should have done a little more work to get here. Hemingway's first sight of Kilimanjaro came after a three-week boat journey from Marseilles, an overnight train ride to Nairobi and two days' driving. And then he fell ill almost immediately, and was forced to return to Nairobi, where, from his hospital bed, he reported back to *Esquire* readers as 'Your amebic dysentery correspondent'.

Symptoms of a.d. run from weakly insidious through spectacular to phenomenal. I believe the record is held by a Mr. McDonald with 232 movements in the twenty-four hours although many old a.d. men claim the McDonald record was never properly audited.

His illness didn't put him off. He was captivated by Africa.

A brown land like Wyoming and Montana but with greater roll and distance ... Nothing that I have ever read has given any idea of the beauty of the country.

What land I can see, beyond the fence of the camp, is studded with thorn trees and a light carpet of grass. The local Masai, unmissable in brightly patterned red cloaks, pass by on their way between the villages.

The abrupt transition from a small crowded country to a big empty one lends an air of unreality which I know will, like altitude sickness, take a day or two to clear.

'In Africa a thing is true at first light and a lie by noon.' Hemingway noted this on his second, longer trip to Africa in the 1950s and for everyone, from pampered tourist to native goat-herder, the hour of dawn is the best time.

It's prime time for Kilimanjaro spotters too. At 6.30, having been woken by the traditional on-safari cup of tea, I stick my head out of the tent and there, so close and so high that I think it must be a cloud formation, is the rim of the great mountain, peeking out above a cornice of dark cloud.

By the time I've found my notebook and pen it's disappeared again. Hemingway complained that on his second trip the mountain didn't show itself for three weeks and I become despondent, but by the time I've dressed and walked up the hill to the spreading timbered and thatch-roofed space where we eat breakfast, the cloud has rolled back to reveal the whole long crest of the mountain, 'as wide as all the world', as Hemingway described it in 'The Snows of Kilimanjaro'. It is an *unbelievably* powerful sight. On the eastern tip of this great ridge a glacier catches the sun.

Hemingway would probably have been out by now and bagged a gazelle or two, but things have changed. Most people who come to Africa nowadays shoot the animals with Leica and Pentax rather than Mannlicher and Browning. National Parks have been created to protect the animals (Amboseli opened soon after Hemingway's last visit) and white hunters have largely been superseded by black rangers and game wardens.

Hemingway, obsessive hunter though he was, was not the kind of sportsman to shoot from cars or hides or after dark when the animals were blinded by powerful lights. For him tracking on foot, using the knowledge of animals inculcated in him by his father and grandfather, was the best and fairest way for a man to hunt.

Today I'm going out into the bush in that spirit, in the company of my two guides, Jackson, a Masai, and Ali, a Kenyan Moslem.

It is the day to christen my Hemingway Jacket, which I spotted in a magazine at the Chicago gun range and which I find is still produced by Willis and Geiger to his original design.

What do I get for my $153? Well, as far as I can gather from the catalogue, a walking munitions dump. 'Added shell pockets, recoil pad, expandable chest pockets, two huge bellowed cargo pockets for shells and a sleeve pocket for shooting glasses.' The last item is a reminder that Hemingway suffered from poor eyesight for most of his life and, before dealing with a charging rhino, had to pop on a pair of little round specs which made him look more like a professor of poetry than a great white hunter.

First we drive a couple of miles or so to Lake Amboseli which, despite a year of drought, still retains water from the El Niño downpours of the year before. The grass cover is still green, and rich stands of vegetation mark fertile lava flows from the mountain.

In the near distance we pass ostriches ruffling their feathers and a pair of zebra mating and the occasional elephant plodding, but the most common beast in the bush is the cow, usually preceded by some solitary walking figure, often no more than a child.

A larger herd of elephant is indicated by footprints on the track, so we climb down off the vehicles and proceed on foot – something generally discouraged amongst tourists.

Jackson wears his Masai cloak, red with yellow stripe, thong sandals, and a coloured bead head-strap. Ali is in his green safari gear.

The presence of any large animals is advertised in advance by numbers of white birds called cattle egrets that ride the big game around with a proprietary air. The bigger and heavier the creature the more the egrets like them, for their feet break up the soil and bring to the surface fresh supplies of the locusts, flies and grasshoppers on which the birds feed.

There are maybe a dozen elephant, including young, making their way slowly towards their next meal. They have almost insatiable appetites. A fully-grown elephant chews up 300 lbs of vegetation and drinks thirty to fifty gallons of water every day, but their metabolism is poor and less than half what they eat is digested. So they make their way across the bush rather like a line of combine harvesters, stuffing it in one end and depositing it, semi-digested, from the other.

Jackson and Ali approach the herd slowly and carefully. Elephants' eyesight, like their digestion, leaves something to be desired. They walk with their head and eyes down and are more likely to see you approach from the back or the side than they are from the front.

Ali says you can get to within a dozen feet of a herd if you're upwind of them. He bends down, picks up a handful of dust and tosses it in the air to see which way the wind is blowing.

As he does so the elephants' ears flap and their highly sensitive trunks are up sniffing for trouble. As there are young with them Ali keeps his distance. I'm not complaining, just watching them is therapeutic. Elephants have a combination of mass and grace that is impressive and compelling. When they are threatened they can transform their bulk to a powerhouse of aggression which, once seen, is something always respected and never forgotten. Even Hemingway would never shoot an elephant.

The lion is another thing altogether.

Being British, we regard the lion as a symbol of pride and invincibility. To the Masai he is Simba, killer of cattle and Public Enemy Number One. Jackson was in his teens when he was one of a group of ten young Masai who confronted a lion and killed it with spears. I ask him from how far away.

He grins. 'As close as possible.'

Which, when pressed, he reckoned to be no more than four feet.

Though the Masai see the lion as a pest, the tourist sees him as a star whom he will pay good money to see. There have been recent moves to try and reconcile these positions. Any agreement ultimately rests on whether the Masai believe they can make enough money from tourism to justify the loss of their cattle.

As we draw a little closer to the swamp, bird life proliferates. The delicately pretty lily-trotter, or African jacana, with its enormous clown's feet, and the black-winged stilt, whose most striking feature is a pair of long, very red legs, pick at the mud with their beaks whilst brown herons and crowned cranes with jazzy yellow crests take a more leisurely approach. Tawny eagles turn and turn above, and swallows, migrated here, like us, from Europe, dart around, low to the ground.

Where there is a stretch of clear water a flock of flamingos has settled. Startled by our approach they peel off into the sky, turning in a perfect curve, wings catching the light. Jackson warns me that snakes like these lakeside conditions. He has seen pythons here and urges me to walk carefully and make heavy footfalls to warn them of my approach. That would be something, a Python killed by a python.

A grazing herd of thirty Cape buffalo regards us warily. These are big animals, weighing in at around 1500 lbs and dangerous. At the back of the herd a buffalo calf is being born. The cow stays standing and as the calf drops to the ground, she turns and begins to lick it extensively and thoroughly, chewing up the placenta. The new-born calf looks around, blinking and startled as if this is the last thing it wanted to happen. Within a couple of minutes it is standing unsteadily, staggering, falling and being urged up again by the mother. Within five minutes it is standing on its own. A domestic calf would take several hours to stand unassisted, but in this hostile environment such helplessness could be fatal.

At the end of the day we climb up to a small steep bluff called Kitirua Hill. Below us the plain is streaked with vivid splashes of crimson and scarlet as columns of Masai herdsmen, driving their cattle before them, return to the *boma*, their encampment, before nightfall.

Ali pours us all beers but this is Ramadan and he cannot take a drink himself until the sun has set.

It dips close to the horizon, but seems to linger there most provocatively.

'Has it gone?' Ali keeps asking anxiously.

Though we tell him it has, near enough, it is not until he's satisfied that the very last trace of the rim has disappeared that he reaches for a bottle of Sprite. It's the first food or drink that has passed his lips since ten o'clock last night.

Back at Tortilis camp, I shower and check myself for ticks. 'Small black things, about this long,' warns Hans, the manager, parting his thumb and forefinger by at least an inch. We're treated to Italian food tonight, dispensed by Jackson, who has traded his Masai cloak for a waiter's black tie.

The exhilaration of a day spent walking in the bush merely confirms that Africa can never be reduced to European intimacy and cosiness. I fall asleep, having struggled to read *Green Hills of Africa* in the dim lamp-light, listening to the birds and bats above me in the thatch and the occasional indefinable grunt or shriek from much further away and the evening wind that grows hour by hour until, in the middle of the night, it suddenly dies and I am woken by total silence.

I'm in a twin-engined Cessna 206, built thirty-one years ago, flying east from Tortilis camp towards a low range called the Chyulu Hills, which lie between the National Parks of Amboseli and Tsavo.

Hemingway knew of Tsavo by reputation, for it was immortalised by one J. H. Patterson in his book *The Man-Eaters of Tsavo*, an account of two lions who preyed on men building the Mombasa–Nairobi railway, eating twenty-eight of them before being caught. The lions' stuffed remains became star exhibits at the Field Museum in Chicago, one of young Ernest's favourite haunts.

Hemingway knew the Chyulu Hills from direct experience, for in his second African trip, in 1953, he stayed close by when he took on the job of Honorary Game Warden. The man who is flying my plane there today, skimming it over a sand-coloured plain sprinkled with zebra and wildebeest and herds of Masai cattle, is the current Honorary Game Warden in the area. His name is Richard Bonham, a Kenyan with an interest in up-market safari lodges. He's short, wiry and weathered and somewhere around fifty, though his outdoor complexion and sun-bleached hair make him look much younger. He's anxious about the fate of two

Masai children and their herd of goats who went missing from their village last night.

He's also very worried about a constipated cheetah, one of a pair which he took in recently after they were orphaned and couldn't hunt.

Once we've touched down he drives me straight to the cage which has been erected for the cheetah in the shade of two tall, isolated trees. The female of the pair escaped only the day before, adding insult to injury for her constipated companion. He looks very sorry for himself, in marked contrast to the chirpy rabbits in cages nearby. They haven't yet worked out that their relationship with the cheetah is purely gastronomic.

Richard beckons me to follow him into the cage.

'They love being stroked,' he says, as if we're going to see a baby kitten. As we approach, the cheetah retreats into the corner, which makes me feel a little better.

'Aim for the top of the head here.' He moves aside to let me have a go.

'Is he tame?' I find myself asking in a curiously husky voice.

'Well, he's *half*-tame.'

'Which half?'

'We didn't want to tame him completely or he won't be able to survive when we turn him loose.'

Oh, great.

'That's good. Approach directly from the front. Let your hand move in a straight line to the top of his head.' My arm suddenly feels very heavy.

The cheetah bares his teeth and backs up. My hand wobbles. I breathe deeply and keep it moving. It's almost there, hovering above the big, sad, yellow eyes, when the cheetah delivers a sharp and wholly unexpected right hook to my leg. I reel back, clutching my calf to stem the blood flow. Sadly, there is no blood, indeed the claw marks are barely visible to the naked eye, but I later note two tiny but unmistakable punctures in my Hugo Boss chinos which bear witness to the fact that I can now add 'Attacked by Cheetah' to my resumé.

Later, at Richard's lodge, Ol Donyo Wuas (which means the Spotted Hills in the Masai language): like Tortilis, this place is constructed with local materials and in local style. One end of my room, cantilevered ten feet or so off the ground, is open to the elements. As we are on the slopes of the hills, the view from my bed is enormous, stretching across the plain to the cloud bank fifty miles away, behind which lurks Kilimanjaro.

It's the magic hour of sunset. Sounds of cow bells and distant voices. I run a shower with water heated by a wood-burning kiln, then sit for a while and watch vervet monkeys watching me from nearby trees. A small herd of hartebeest springs out of the bushes and stops, warily, to munch the grass in the clearing below me. Examine my cheetah wound and for an embarrassing moment cannot even remember which leg it's on.

Woken, with tea, at twenty past five. Dawn comes like an old television set warming up. Every time I look outside there's a little more light in the darkness. By six-thirty we have the full picture and Kilimanjaro is clear enough for Richard to suggest we fly out to the mountain and get our pictures as soon as possible. By ten o'clock it will be hidden again.

As we drive down to the airstrip at the bottom of the hill the cattle are being moved out of the *bomas* to catch the morning dew on the grass. The Masai way of life looks idyllic on this dry, sun-sharpened morning, but Richard says it is much more like the Wild West than it looks. Twenty per cent of the Masai own seventy per cent of the cattle. These cattle barons are rich by African standards, some owning a truck or even a tractor.

Once we're airborne we head south-east across grass so dry it seems to take on the colour and texture of sand. This prairie soon gives way to green scrub and thorn tree cover, but as the mountain comes nearer, the landscape changes with dramatic speed from lush, tropical farmland through rainforest to timber plantations, moorland and eventually alpine desert. The transitions are fast and exhilarating, but not without a cost. As we rise through ten thousand feet I feel the disadvantages of an unpressurised cabin: shortage of breath, difficulty in writing, a touch of nausea.

We shall never be able to fly high enough to look down on the mountain (it's just short of twenty thousand feet, and the safe operating altitude for our two small planes is no more than fifteen), but we're close enough to see vivid detail.

In geological terms Kilimanjaro is a baby, formed by massive volcanic activity less than a million years ago, and far from extinct. On closer examination it is in fact two mountains in one, the wide table-top dome, called Kibo, and on the eastern edge, the much more jagged and dramatic outline of Mawenzi, with sheer sides and precipitous plunging crevasses. The north face of Kibo rises steep, black and fissured to the highest point on the African continent. A glacier runs down from the summit and I can see thick snow walls. It was in these snows that the carcass of a leopard was found in the 1920s.

No one knows what the leopard was doing at such an altitude, but the legend inspired 'The Snows of Kilimanjaro', one of Hemingway's finest short stories.

Not that Richard regards the story as legend. He says his father pointed out the bones of the leopard when he took him up the mountain as a child. If we have time he can show me the remains of a Dakota aircraft that smashed into the side of

Mawenzi with a valuable haul of emeralds on board. Part of the fuselage still hangs there, and no one has yet been able to reach the emeralds.

One man recently hauled himself up to the top of Kilimanjaro to attempt the world para-gliding record.

'And did he do it?'

Richard makes a quick adjustment to keep us alongside the camera plane.

'He was never seen again.'

By now the cloud is rolling up the walls of Kilimanjaro like a shroud and there is no time for Dakotas or emeralds. By ten o'clock it has enveloped us and the mountain might just as well not be there.

Richard turns the Cessna and heads back across the plain. On the way home he takes me low over game grazing on the salt licks and skims the tops of the acacia orchard where the white rhino which Hemingway hunted were once found in abundance. Now they're virtually gone. Poachers have reduced their numbers from several hundred to six, maybe ten. The demand from Asia for rhino horn has killed its source.

Richard raises his voice over the noise of the engine, 'The days of the wild rhino are over. Finished.'

Back on the ground he's rewarded with the news that the two Masai children are safe. Their goats did a runner in the night and they went after them. But there are other headaches for the Honorary Game Warden. Cattle poachers are laying traps in the hills and he will have to take a group of rangers to investigate.

When Hemingway first came to Africa in 1933, the idea of him becoming a game warden was faintly ludicrous. His wife Pauline's diary of that trip hardly reveals a conservationist at work: 'They killed four Thompson gazelle, eight Grant, seven wildebeest, seven impala, two klipspringers, four roan, two bushbucks, three reedbucks, two oryx, four topi, two water-buck, one eland and three kudu. Of dangerous game, they killed their licensed limit: four lions, three cheetahs, four buffalo, two leopards and two rhinos. They also killed one serval cat, two warthogs, thirteen zebra and one cobra. For amusement forty-one hyenas were also killed.'

Twenty years later Hemingway, though famous enough to be gratefully offered the title of Game Warden, was less desperate for trophies. And there were other diversions. He became infatuated with a girl called Debba, from the Wakaba tribe. She and he canoodled and at one time broke Mary's bed when she was away. There are rumours, only partly cleared up by *True at First Light*, that they may even have undergone a sort of marriage ceremony.

I think of this as Richard shows me lethal cattle traps of tree trunk and coils of wire left by today's Wakamba who kill the trapped cattle and ship the meat back over the hills to their territory.

As Richard and his rangers dismantle the traps he tells me that poachers would not have been called poachers in Hemingway's time. What the Wakamba were doing then was practising the right to hunt, part of a long and ancient tradition. Now the law has separated them from their hunting grounds without recompense and without an alternative way of life. The traps are cruel but almost inevitable. Rivalry with the neighbouring two tribes has always been intense. They have always been different, the Wakamba hunting with bows and arrows, the Masai with spears (which they cannot make for themselves, they are forged by another tribe on the foot-hills of Kilimanjaro).

In *True at First Light*, Hemingway, even allowing for a bit of romantic bias, has his own characteristic views on what makes the Wakamba different.

Their warriors had always fought in all of Britain's wars and the Masai had never fought in any. The Masai had been coddled, preserved, treated with a fear that they should never have inspired and been adored by all the homosexuals ... who had worked for the Empire in Kenya and Tanganyika because the men were so beautiful ... The Wakamba hated the Masai as rich show-offs protected by the government.

In the evening, back at Ol Donyo Wuas, it's chilly enough for a log fire. As we discuss the sort of day we've all had, Alex, the young Englishman who runs the lodge, rolls up his sleeve to show a mass of claw marks, sustained whilst trying to befriend the constipated cheetah.

Maybe I should look at my wound again. With a stronger magnifying glass.

In the middle of the night I'm woken by the sound of light scuttling, followed by a crash and the rapid dripping of water on to my suitcase. I feel around blearily beneath the pillow, find my torch and shine the beam through the mosquito net in the direction of the noise.

A few feet away, on the wooden work-top that runs at the back of the cabin, a furry creature with a beautiful black and white striped tail is lapping away at a small pool of water. It carries on quite unconcerned until I utter a grunt of indignation, at which it flits away behind the cupboard, where it hides very badly, leaving most of its tail sticking out.

I tell the story at breakfast and Alex shakes his head with mild exasperation.

'It's the genet again,' he says, as if it had been an ant on the toothbrush. 'Large-spotted genet. They love the water, you see. We put covers on top but they just take them off and tip the jug over.'

While I'm mulling this over, Richard arrives in a state of great elation. He's just heard that the cheetah has had a movement.

Things continue in this visceral vein as he tells us that he is on his way to the local village to attend a circumcision ceremony and would we like to come along.

Well, there's nothing on television, so why not.

As we climb into the Land Rovers and head off up the hill through trees and green meadows Richard fills me in on the background. Circumcision, both male and female, is still practised by the local Masai. For the boys it is seen as a rite of passage, part of the process of becoming a man, and the operation is not performed until they are in their teens.

It is all done to a carefully prescribed ritual. The circumcision itself takes place, like so much else in Africa, at first light, and outside the main entrance to the *boma*. By the time we arrive it is already underway. A group of six or seven young men surround the boy whose body looks limp and inert beneath a loose black robe. A man in an old coat and a Kenya Tea Company sports hat is kneeling before him. This is the surgeon. His knives and some antiseptic spirit are in a filthy old box beside him.

There is no sound from the boy as, clutching his penis, he is carried back into the compound by his friends and into one of the low mud huts. It is considered to be very important not to cry out or acknowledge the pain. This restraint is known as *emorata* – what Hemingway might have called 'grace under pressure' – and is part of what makes a boy into a *moran*, a warrior.

The Masai are nomadic and this *boma* is a temporary refuge for thirty families, some hundred and eighty people, who are joined at night by their livestock. The floor is a soft layer of trodden animal dung. Clouds of flies gather instantly at mouth, nose and eyes.

Three young warriors, only a little older than the boy, select a cow and fire an arrow into its jugular, swiftly placing a gourd beneath the wound to draw off blood. A coagulant on the tip of the arrow seals the incision and not a drop of unwanted blood is spilled. The gourd is carried across to the boy's hut, where his mother mixes it with milk into a pink slurry, the colour of strawberry yoghurt, which is taken indoors to be drunk by her son.

I am asked into the hut, an invitation which I accept rather gingerly. Bending double, I stoop my way along the short curved tunnel of an entrance and find myself confronted by a scene of unexpected serenity, a bit like a nativity. The mother and grandmother sit beside the fire and the boy is lying silently beneath a rough cloth blanket to one side. Only the tossing and turning of his head indicates what he is going through. The women smile in welcome, and one of them moves to the boy's bed and pulls the blanket closer around his shoulders. He will stay here for two weeks.

Outside, the young men are lighting a fire by spinning an acacia stick on to a base of cedar. I notice that one of them has a little trouble as his Rolex watch keeps sliding down. It takes ten minutes or more before a little smoke appears, although they break off frequently to be photographed.

Though the Masai in general, and the women in particular, seem to resent the camera, these young boys will pose at the drop of a hat. They may look warlike but it's all a bit of a put-on. Their faces are beautifully painted, their hair elaborately hennaed, their ear lobes cut and shaped to take a dazzling array of adornment, their beads and bracelets and rich red tunics artfully arranged. Small hand-mirrors hang from straps on their waist.

One of the boys speaks good English. Instead of sending him out with the cattle his father sent him to the local school.

He says it is very important to look beautiful.

'Who is the most beautiful here?' I ask, hoping to stir up a little local rivalry. It backfires.

He indicates several of his companions, 'We are all beautiful.' Then he turns back to me. 'Except you!' He breaks into a toothy grin, the others into fits of giggles.

In the background I see the old man who circumcised the boy weaving unsteadily amongst the huts. He is rewarded for his work with as much beer as he can drink and already has the third or fourth bottle of Tusker at his lips. No one talks to him. I ask an older Masai about him. He says that circumcision is always done by the poorest people, usually from another village.

'Is he good?'

My friend is philosophical. 'Some are good, some are bad.'

His own circumcision took over an hour. He nods across to the hut where the boy lies. 'He'll be all right in five days.'

In *True at First Light*, as they sit outside their mess tent feeling the cool night breeze off Mount Kilimanjaro, Miss Mary (Mary Hemingway), tells the narrator (Ernest):

'I want to go and really see something of Africa. We'll be going home and we haven't seen anything. I want to see the Belgian Congo.'

'I don't.'

'You don't have any ambition. You'd just as soon stay in one place.'

'Have you ever been in a better place?'

It's easy to imagine the real life Hemingways having this conversation as they looked out on Kilimanjaro, the way we do this morning. Right now, as a soft wind blows and the dust rises from the cattle trudging across this magnificent wide-screen landscape, I would back Ernest. I have been in few better places.

But Miss Mary was a tenacious woman and eventually got what she wanted.

On 21 January 1954 the Hemingways, with a bush pilot by the name of Roy Marsh, took off from Nairobi to see the Belgian Congo. Hemingway called it his Christmas present to Mary.

After flying due north to look down on friends in the rich farming belt of the Kenya Highlands they turned south, inspecting the lakes and volcanoes of the Great Rift Valley, the twelve-mile-wide Ngorongoro Crater and the game-filled Serengeti Plains. After a refuelling stop at Mwanza they headed west, out over Lake Victoria and the desolate northern quarter of Rwanda and by the end of the first day they reached the Belgian Congo, putting down for the night at the town of Costermansville, now Bukavu.

The next day they flew north over the Rwenzori mountains, a spectacular snow-capped range in the very centre of Africa, known to early explorers as the Mountains of the Moon, and from there to Entebbe in Uganda. Hemingway, in his article 'The Christmas Gift', for *Look* magazine, extravagantly praised the comforts of Entebbe's Lake Victoria Hotel, adding pointedly that he hoped 'Miss Mary was beginning to lose the claustrophobia she had experienced while being confined to the Masai Reserve and the slopes of Mount Kilimanjaro.'

But Miss Mary's claustrophobia was far from cured and once the mist cleared next morning they were in the air again heading over George and Albert, the lakes of the Western Rift Valley, and on to the Murchison Falls on the River Nile. Diving down to what Hemingway later described as 'a reasonably legal height', they had a good look at this spectacular torrent of white water, and were heading back to Entebbe when their tail and propeller clipped a telegraph wire and the plane hurtled down into low scrub beside the crocodile-infested waters of the Nile. This was only the start of the nightmare.

I suppose you could say it's because of Mary that we find ourselves uprooted from our earthly paradise beside Kilimanjaro, flown north-west across the Equator and deposited, at the end of a long day, in the sticky humidity of lakeside Entebbe. No genets at night, no cups of tea to wake us in the morning, just the putrid stink of corridors sprayed against the ubiquitous lake flies, and a lavatory cistern that shoots a jet of water onto my head whenever I pull the chain.

A terrific din wakens me. Cannot immediately distinguish the sound. Is it a hurricane or is the building collapsing? It turns out to be thick plummeting rain, drumming on the ground and on the roof, product of a massive tropical storm.

The prospect of a light plane trip in the morning makes me anxious. Pad off to the lavatory. Water on my head again.

On our way to Entebbe airport we are flagged down at a checkpoint. Two security men step out from beside a large notice warning 'Please Deposit Firearms, Briefcases'.

They examine our mini-bus, especially the bulky camera equipment inside. Whilst one walks alongside with a strange coat-hanger device held in front of him, his colleague questions us.

'Anything to declare?'

'No.'

'No guns?'

'No. No guns.'

He seems quite taken by surprise and repeats our answer incredulously. 'No *guns*?'

I rather feel we've let him down.

By the time our two single-engined Cessnas take off, the worst of the storm has passed, but an hour out of Entebbe we hit a belt of heavy rain at seven thousand feet. The little plane bucks alarmingly and water streaks across the window below which I can see the outline of our right-hand landing wheel, and far below it occasional glimpses of great curved rocks rising from dense tropical forest. The weather is so bad that we have to put down at a maize-field airstrip close by a game lodge called Semliki, on the edge of the Mountains of the Moon.

In grand comfort, under a tall thatch roof, we have lunch and, after the rain passes, set off again, flying north. The long thin finger of Lake Albert separates Uganda from what is now the Republic of the Congo. The Congo shore is hidden in a haze of smoke from land-burning fires, but the eastern shore of the lake is clear. A long cliff wall folds gracefully down to the water as the escarpment meets the Western Rift Valley. Waterfalls cascade down the rock-face splashing onto narrow beach settlements, inaccessible from the landward side. Fishermen's boats are drawn up on the shore and the huts are simple straw shelters. As we fly lower and closer I'm surprised to see these tiny villages are full of people. They wave up at us and the children caper around as we fly over them. The sun breaks through for the first time today, sending an imprint of our fragile little plane skimming across the waters below.

At the head of Lake Albert, on its eastern shore, is our first sight of the Nile, snaking east and north, a coil of silver in the late afternoon sun. When we get closer I can see large herds of elephant in the shallows, and the heads of innumerable basking hippos. Fish-eagles looking like lords in ermine with their white head and neck feathers fly below us as we slowly descend toward the falls.

The Murchison Falls are not high and they're so enclosed in rocks and forest that you don't see them until you're almost on top of them. What makes them so special is the sheer power of the water-flow. This is no elegant sheet of falling water, it's more like a power-jet. The Nile, a third of a mile wide as it flows off the plateau, is squeezed into a tortuous gorge only twenty or thirty yards across. Some of the water spills over a precipice further away, but the bulk of this throttled river blasts its way downwards in a corkscrew spiral, the water tossed from one rock face to another until it crashes out of the gorge in a carpet of foam a quarter of a mile wide and half a mile long.

We land at a dirt airstrip nearby then take the ferry over the river to put up for the night at the Nile Safari Camp.

There is no respite from the heat, no evening breeze like the one that cooled us in the Chyulu Hills. Instead, the chatter of crickets and the drone of mosquitoes and, echoing up from the river below, a frog chorus interspersed with the chuckle and splash of the hippos.

When the Hemingways passed their unscheduled night in the undergrowth beside Murchison Falls, with Mary in considerable pain, they spent it building fires and scaring off elephants whilst Roy Marsh sent out Mayday signals and desperately repeated the plane's call sign: 'Victor Love Item! Victor Love Item!'

The call didn't reach the crew of a BOAC Argonaut which flew over the scene, reported seeing wreckage and presumed whoever was down there was dead. They didn't know it was Ernest Hemingway, and he was already making survival plans.

We rationed the Carlsberg beer, which was to be consumed at the rate of one bottle each two days shared among three people. We rationed the Grand MacNish [whisky] which was to be issued one drink each evening. The water we planned to renew from the Murchison Falls where there seemed to be a plentiful supply.

'A Christmas Gift'

A local man named Francis Oyoo Okot, who works for the Uganda Wildlife Service, says he knows exactly where the Hemingways' plane came down. His father had shown it to him when he was ten years old, which must make Francis, a gentle beaming man, almost my own age. The site is a mile or two up-stream from our camp and he takes me there in a converted Lake Albert fishing-boat, called *Overtime*, for reasons I can't quite work out.

Shoals of leathery pink hippo lie in the water in family groups, some with only their ears and eyeballs above the water. They snort, propel themselves gently about and occasionally get into a short-lived scrap, but basically they lie there in the shallows exuding a placid atmosphere of deep, vaguely erotic contentment.

We pass the time talking of our families. It's a rather one-sided conversation as Francis has twelve children to my three. When I ask him their ages his brow furrows.

'The oldest is twenty-two and the next ...' His voice tails off apologetically. 'Well, there are so many.'

He has been working for the park service for over thirty years and his activities have not been confined to boat trips and bird-spotting. He has three gun-shot wounds from run-ins with poaching gangs. He pulls up his shirt and rolls up his yellow trousers to show me the scars. One bullet is still embedded in his left thigh.

We turn into a small bay about a mile down-stream from the falls, passing uncomfortably close to a rock entirely covered by the largest, most evil-looking crocodile I've ever seen. Two or three persistent kingfishers dive-bomb the frothy water around us as we pull into the shore.

As we disembark and make for the thick and thorny undergrowth, I notice for the first time that Francis' injury causes him to limp quite badly. But he pushes on with gusto, knocking aside the branches until we come across a telegraph pole, abandoned and weathered to the colour of the undergrowth around it. This, he tells me, is the remains of the old telegraph line that brought down the Hemingways. After more cutting and slashing we break through into an open sandy area at the bottom of a rocky cliff where the plane actually came to rest.

There were many more elephants around then and the area would have been much less thickly wooded.

Francis leads me to the top of a rocky outcrop, a climb of about a hundred and fifty feet. The morning after the crash Hemingway and the pilot carried Mary up here to avoid the elephants and it was from this bluff that they first saw the approach of a sight-seeing launch, the SS *Murchison*, which was carrying a party celebrating a golden wedding. The son-in-law proved to be a surgeon, who diagnosed Mary as having two broken ribs. The boat proved to be the one on which Katharine Hepburn and Humphrey Bogart filmed *The African Queen*, and best of all, for Hemingway, it boasted 'An excellent refrigerator containing Tusker beer and several brands of ale'.

Francis and I slowly make our way down to the beach from which the Hemingway party was rescued. I ask him if there is anything left here from the accident – an unpublished novel perhaps. He smiles and shakes his head. Everything was collected and taken down to Butiaba, which is where we have to go if we want to know more about the saga of Miss Mary's Christmas present.

A terrifying cry rends the night air. A harsh and fearful screech, repeated three or four times until the noise dies to a whimper. I lie, frozen sleepless and full of awful imaginings. Something torn from the trees by a creature from the river. Fighting to get away.

Despite the fact that modern man was born in the cradle of these African Rift Valleys, mortality, of one kind or another, always feels close at hand in Africa. Maybe that's why Hemingway liked it, student of death that he was.

I'm idiotically keen on keeping things alive. It probably comes from some deep need to be liked, even by ants and bluebottles.

I remember once in India seeing a naked man, surrounded by a small crowd, being escorted down a street in Delhi. I assumed he'd been arrested for indecent exposure. It turned out that he was a religious leader, a holy man of the Jainists who believe in non-injury of living things. If he dressed then there would be the danger of his clothes squashing some tiny creatures. They call this practice *Ahimsa*.

All this weighs on my mind for two or three seconds, then I fall back to sleep until five o'clock, when I wake to find a bat flying around in my tent. Unzip the front flap, but for all their much-vaunted powers of radar, it takes fifteen minutes for the bat to find its way out.

We are into our vehicles and off towards Butiaba even before the party of Austrians who arrived last night has stirred. The road is so bad that we have made little progress by sunrise. Outside one village we pull to a halt, beguiled by the sight of a woman, in a T-shirt and brightly patterned skirt, striding through the fields carrying a bale of cotton on her head. Our local assistant approaches her, tells her we are from the BBC and would she mind if we filmed her as she walked.

At which moment heads pop up from all over the long grass and before we know it the fields are alive with the sound of directors.

'Do it once more! They want you to do it once more!' the ever-growing crowd shouts at the hapless woman.

'You must walk faster! You must walk more slowly!'

The pitted mud road tips and sways us on between fields of maize and sweet potato, trees crowded with black kites, and Manhattan-like termite mounds over ten feet high.

The town of Masindi, where we arrive mid-morning, is the administrative centre for the region and its dusty pot-holed streets are lively. The buildings are single-storey and some are laid out with steps and shaded arcades which bear the names of the Asian shopkeepers who built them and who were later ordered out of Uganda by Idi Amin. The current President, Museveni, is encouraging them back.

Masindi offers a rich variety of products and services. One shop advertises the 'Mandela' Human Love Charm, another, 'Good Morning' Lung Tonic. There are businesses like The Honest Brothers – Dealers In Essential Commodities, 'In God We Trust' Electrical Suppliers and Wiring, and the alarmingly candid New Fracture Driving School.

Lured by the sign outside the Bamugisa Barber Shop, which 'Cares To Make You Smat', I go inside for a trim.

So pleased is Fredrick Magembe with the job he does that he insists I have my portrait painted so he can add it to the display board outside the shop. I am greatly honoured to be chosen to represent style Number 8 at the Bamugisa Barber Shop in Masindi.

We spend the night at the old railway hotel. It is basic. Inside, a narrow bed, with no mosquito net and lots of mosquitoes, bare bulbs and dodgy wiring. Outside, a long verandah and a spreading jacaranda with copious blue blossom. We're sitting out here at the end of the day, trying to find the cool breeze, when a group of curious and very polite schoolchildren come by. One of them, who cannot be more than ten, regards me for a moment and says, solemnly:

'We are here to make friends.'

*

Butiaba is an hour's drive from Masindi. It's a spectacular drive, over the escarpment, past a memorial to the Scottish engineer who laid out the road and who was trampled to death by an elephant for his pains.

The air on top is fresh and invigorating. By the time we have wound our way down to Butiaba it's hot and listless. The town is low and scattered and poor, its limited resources strained by a steady influx of refugees fleeing from the unrest in the Congo, twenty-five miles away across the lake. The livelihood is fishing and as we get there the morning boats are coming in and most of the town, as well as their goats, cows and thin bleating sheep, is gathered at the beach.

As soon as the catch is landed the women slit and gut the fish, mostly Nile perch and the smaller tiger fish, and set them out to dry on racks. Directing operations is a genial middle-aged Ugandan wearing a striped shirt, thick brown trousers and bright blue rubber boots. His name is Abdul. He is one of the village elders and he knows where we can find the last piece of Hemingway's Ugandan jigsaw. By the time the SS *Murchison* had brought the party safely to Butiaba, word had gone out, via the wire-services of the world, that one of the greatest living authors (*The Old Man and the Sea* had just won a Pulitzer Prize) was missing, believed dead, in the heart of Africa. Bounty-hunters were already searching the area and the lucky one, a Captain Reginald Cartwright, had tracked them to Butiaba. He had a de Havilland Rapide refuelled and ready to whisk them out of this hell-hole and back to Entebbe.

Hemingway was not so keen and felt that he would rather proceed by road, but he was overruled and the three of them – Ernest, Mary and Roy Marsh, the pilot of the plane that had just crashed – squeezed into the Rapide.

Hemingway described for *Look* magazine readers what happened next.

One third of the way down the alleged airstrip, I was convinced that we would not be airborne successfully. However, we continued at the maximum rate of progress of the aircraft which was leaping from crag to crag ... in the manner of the wild goat. Suddenly, this object ... became violently air-borne through no fault of its own. This condition existed only for a matter of seconds after which the aircraft became violently de-air-borne and there was the usual sound, with which we were all by now familiar, of rending metal.

The tone of Hemingway's casually flippant description doesn't accord with what Abdul remembers of the aftermath of Reggie Cartwright's failed take-off.

Standing amongst grazing cows in the wispy grassland which, apart from a rusted pole on which a wind-direction arrow still turns, is all that remains of Butiaba airstrip. Abdul remembers seeing the pilot climbing in, last of them all.

'He was just a young boy,' he says, as if by way of explanation.

He confirms that the plane took off, 'just a little way, then landed again,' hitting the ground, bursting the right wing tank and beginning to burn. Mr Hemingway was the last to come out of the plane (thinking he was trapped he'd head-butted a door open).

Abdul frowns in concentration.

'He came running towards us. His hair was on fire and he was crying.'

Abdul beckons us to follow him through the yellowing grass to a point beneath a solitary goblet-shaped cactus tree they call a euphorbia. This is where the plane came down and this is where Abdul found pieces of the wreckage, some of which he has kept. He shows me parts of a cylinder, a battery and torn shreds of fuselage fabric. I ask him if anyone has ever shown any interest in these relics of one of Hemingway's most serious accidents. He shakes his head. No one has been out here.

I look around. The wind-direction arrow squeaks and read-justs itself, the only landmark in the featureless bush. It's hard to think that anything important ever happened here.

Hemingway's survival of two consecutive air crashes was news across the world, and generally the cause of much rejoicing. But it had come at considerable cost. Writing to Harvey Breit ten days later Hemingway assessed the damage.

I ruptured the kidneys, or maybe only one, the liver, the spleen (whoever she is) had the brain fluid ooze out to soak the pillow every night, burnt the top of the scalp off, etc. Also ... had to take two breathes in the fire which is something that never really helped anybody except of course Joan Of Arc.

He didn't mention the sprained arm and leg and the crushed vertebrae and the paralysed sphincter and the temporary loss of hearing and eyesight.

We return to Masindi. Maybe it's hearing the story of the crash that has darkened my mood, but I begin to notice the crueller side of life out here. Scrawled on the door of a house just outside the town is a slash of civil war graffiti. 'Bondo Killers Boys', it reads, 'No Living – Child Rat Dog.'

That night a man comes to see me. He is called Ibrahim Bilal and he wears a pink knitted hat and sports a single very prominent white tooth. He and his friend speak Arabic. He worked for Ugandan Railways and remembers being sent from Kampala, the Ugandan capital, to Butiaba in January of 1954 to bring back an important group of Americans, one of whom was badly hurt.

He drove them back to Kampala in a Ford Zephyr staff car, with room for seven people, with a Ugandan, Dr Cabreta, in attendance. One of the men lay on a mattress in the back. Yes, Ibrahim remembers, he was in a serious condition.

'Some of the time he was in agony.'

Appallingly enough, Africa had not finished with Hemingway. A couple of weeks later, recovering at a camp on the Kenya coast at Shimoni, he tried to help deal with a bush-fire nearby and fell into the flames. He suffered second and third degree burns.

We leave Entebbe for London tomorrow. The bad weather has cleared, the oppressive humidity lifted and, after bone-rattling rides through the bush, the pool at the Lake Victoria Hotel looks inviting.

Though we've not been here long it seems like a lifetime. Africa has a way of imposing its own time scale, reducing our busy western lives to its own pace, its own stately rhythm. In Africa the concept of the eternal seems much more meaningful. It also allows you more time to take things in. Events become clearer and impressions sharper and memories more indelible.

Perhaps that's the way it was for Hemingway. He spent less than ten months of his life in Africa and yet from it came two books (one, admittedly, posthumous) and two of his greatest short stories – 'The Snows of Kilimanjaro' and 'The Short Happy Life of Francis Macomber'.

Life in Key West and Cuba may have been safer, but never as intense.

KEY WEST

OPPOSITE TOP RIGHT: Period postcard of the railroad which was destroyed by a hurricane in 1935.

OPPOSITE CENTRE: Modern tourist development. Mallory Square, Key West.

OPPOSITE BELOW: Seven Mile Bridge carries the Overseas Highway through the coral islands of the Florida Keys.

OPPOSITE TOP LEFT: Marlin, the best game fish in the world, drew Hemingway to Key West.

TOP & ABOVE: The newest Sloppy Joe's celebrates Hemingway's 100th anniversary.

RIGHT: Extra large security measures inside Sloppy Joe's.

OPPOSITE ABOVE: Shine Forbes, the man who slugged Hemingway and lived to tell the tale, shows me some of Hemingway's tricks.
OPPOSITE BELOW: Shine's front room, an Aladdin's cave collected over eighty-three years.
ABOVE: Bill Clinton the seven-toed cat at the Hemingway house (below).
RIGHT: Local aficionado at the Hemingway Look-Alike competition.

The men who would be Ernest. Kevin the cop (top row, extreme left) and the Look-Alike class of '99. Winner gets to wear a medal inscribed 'In Papa We Trust'. The winner was local boy 'Big Rick' Kirvan, bottom row extreme right.

OVERLEAF: Schmoozing with the judges.

AFRICA

RIGHT: Big game drew Hemingway to Africa in the 1930s.

CENTRE & BELOW: His old stamping ground is now Amboseli National Park, Kenya. Seeing game on foot is not an option for most tourists, but it was the way Hemingway preferred to do it. Thanks to my trusty escorts, Ali in the cap and Jackson in the Masai robe, I see more than most visitors to these plains.

OPPOSITE TOP: The green hills of Africa – wooded slopes of the Chyulu Hills as seen from Ol Donyo Wuas. In the distance, a panorama of dry plains, dust rising from an approaching vehicle. Somewhere beyond that lurks the tallest mountain in Africa.

ABOVE: The inspiring first sight of Kilimanjaro from a light plane. Kibo, the 19,340-foot summit, is on the right.
LEFT: With Richard Bonham (like Hemingway, an Honorary Game Warden), taking a look at the constipated cheetah. When it's well enough Richard will release it back into the wild. It's 'half-tame' according to Richard, but it turns half-wild when I try to pat it on the head.

The day of a circumcision ceremony at a Masai village.
ABOVE: The grandmother of the circumcised boy mixes blood and milk outside his hut.
BELOW: Blood is taken from one of the cows.
RIGHT: Lighting a fire with sticks for the feast later in the day.

OPPOSITE ABOVE: Comedy spear-throwing. Young Masai warriors cracking up.
OPPOSITE BELOW: Inside the hut: grandmother and mother tend to the boy (behind the curtain) who will take two weeks to recover.

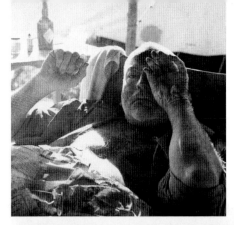

LEFT: Hemingway after the second crash, when he suffered burns and internal injuries from which he never fully recovered.
CENTRE: On the Nile Francis picks his way through dangerous whirlpools and foam from the falls ahead.
BELOW: Butiaba: at the site of Hemingway's second air crash in two days. With Abdul and pieces of the wreckage.

OPPOSITE TOP: Rescuers at the Hemingways' plane after it crash-landed beside the Murchison Falls, Uganda.
OPPOSITE CENTRE: Hemingway made camp on high ground beside the Nile to avoid local wildlife, such as sunbathing crocodile.
OVERLEAF: At barber's shop in Masindi I have a style, Number 8, named after me. On-the-spot portrait makes me look startlingly like Colonel Gaddafi.

CUBA

ABOVE: Havana hand.
RIGHT: The city is a transport time warp. I'm riding a motorcycle side-car taxi.
BELOW: Private cars are a luxury and so there's plenty of room for pedestrians on Havana's famous seafront thoroughfare, the Malecón.

TOP: American cars seem to have survived Castro's Communist revolution, though many of them now have Russian engines. Alfredo (filling the tank) remembers seeing Hemingway driving through Havana in a jeep.

ABOVE & RIGHT: Hemingway sits between his fourth wife, Mary, and Spencer Tracy at the Floridita, his favourite Havana hostelry. The daiquiri was its speciality, but Hemingway insisted on a stronger version which they called the *Papa Doble*.

RIGHT: Forty years on Hemingway's gone, but the *Papa Doble* lives on.

The Finca Vigía, 'Look-Out Farm', Hemingway's Cuban home for twenty years.
RIGHT: One of the sacred typewriters being lovingly cleaned by the staff.
CENTRE: Hemingway on the driveway followed by one of the fifty-seven cats. The house was found for him by his third wife, Martha Gellhorn.

LEFT: Hemingway's favourite boat, the *Pilar*, enshrined in the grounds of Finca Vigía. He left it to his captain Gregorio Fuentes, who in turn left it to the government.
OPPOSITE: On the outside looking in. Because of the delicate state of Hemingway's perfectly preserved possessions you have to be stuffed, or working for the BBC, to get inside the house.

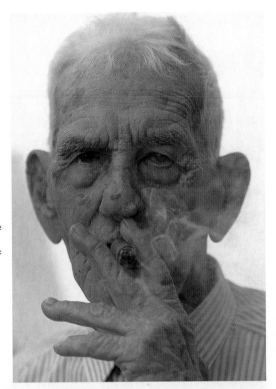

OPPOSITE LEFT: Hemingway working the Gulf Stream. **OPPOSITE ABOVE:** Memorial on the waterfront at Cojímar is a tribute from the locals. **OPPOSITE CENTRE:** A concrete fisherman in the grounds of 'The Old Man and the Sea' Hotel, Marina Hemingway. **OPPOSITE BELOW:** No marlin today, which is why they call it fishing, not catching. **ABOVE:** A luckier fisherman. **RIGHT & BELOW:** Gregorio Fuentes, 101, tells me of the heydays with Hemingway at Cojímar (overleaf) where Hemingway kept his boat.

AMERICAN WEST

LEFT: Bison herds were once so big that it took early explorers ten days to ride through them. Now the sight of a solitary bison brings cars to a halt on the road.
CENTRE: Yellowstone National Park. Thermal energy bubbles up at Fountain Paint Pot.
BELOW: Pre-hunting breakfast at the Corral Bar. The men talk of the liberties and responsibilities of the hunter. These are not trophy hunters; they may take days to stalk one elk.

OPPOSITE PAGE: The Big Country. My first time in Montana and Wyoming and I feel swallowed up by the landscape. **OPPOSITE ABOVE:** Montana; rolling, uninhibited and expansive country.
OPPOSITE BELOW: My one-ton Ford pick-up truck is dwarfed by the forests of Yellowstone National Park, scorched by the huge fires of 1988.

ABOVE: The first time I've felt comfortable on a horse. Riding a Palomino at the Hargrave Ranch, Montana.
LEFT: A bison for the wall at the taxidermist in Outlaw Drive.
BELOW: The front office and recent clients (including stuffed author).

ABOVE: Leo and Ellen – our heavenly hosts at the Hargrave Ranch.

LEFT: 'Wrist and elbow'. All you need to remember when throwing a lasso, according to Ken, my rope coach.

BELOW: The Magnificent Six bring the cattle back home. Less of a stampede, more like rounding up a crèche. But it *was* our first day.

Hemingway's last home, in Ketchum, Idaho.
BELOW: Tragic history but a magnificent setting. Clouds rise over the Sawtooth Mountains to the north.
RIGHT: The sitting-room at night. With big picture window and stairway to bedroom at right of fireplace.

RIGHT: Late daylight spills on to the entrance porch where Hemingway took his own life on 2 July 1961.

ABOVE: Hemingway's physical and mental health deteriorated fast in his last years out west.
LEFT: Wrought-iron work above gates of Ketchum cemetery.
OVERLEAF: The end of the journey. Hemingway's grave at Ketchum. Mary, his wife for fifteen years, lies beside him under the spruce trees.

CUBA

On 28 March 1928, Hemingway wrote to his new
wife Pauline from the Royal Mail steam packet
Orita, westbound from La Rochelle:
'We are five or ten days out on our trip or tripe
to Cuba ... I have often wondered what I should
do with the rest of my life and now I know – I
shall try and reach Cuba.'

Though the letter was mainly a moan about the
slow progress and lack of creature comforts aboard
the **Orita** it was oddly prescient. Twelve years
later, with the help of Martha Gellhorn, his third
wife, Hemingway bought a house in a village on
the outskirts of Havana in which he lived for the
next twenty years – the most permanent home of
his life.

I'd never been to Cuba until Hemingway lured
me there in August and September, the hottest
months of the year and the start of the hurricane
season.

At José Martí International Airport, Havana, jets are climbing into the sky above the gleaming façade of the brand new air-conditioned terminal but I'm in the car park, where the unconditioned air is 34 degrees centigrade and I'm leaning up against the side of a truck for some shade.

My bags are in the taxi, whose back axle is hoisted up on one side whilst our driver struggles to replace a flat tyre. The vehicle looks undignified, like a dog with its leg up.

If I'd wanted to get an instant flavour of what Havana was like in Hemingway's time, they could not have done much better than finding me this beleaguered but handsome tangerine Plymouth, which dates from 1951 – the year he was writing *The Old Man and the Sea*. Even if it does have a 1960s Russian engine.

When we eventually hit the road and turn on to a wide, empty highway outside the airport, almost the first thing I see is a faded billboard advertising the Floridita bar, with Hemingway's countenance sending out a broad, if unconvincing, smile of welcome.

I sink back into the leather seat with a delicious feeling of anticipation. It doesn't last long. Half-way into Havana we hit the road again, only literally this time. There is a dull thud from under my seat and the Plymouth lurches painfully as the replacement tyre explodes, and the car slews round on its wheel rim before coming to a halt beside an embarrassingly crowded bus stop.

No one bats an eyelid. Not a hint of amusement, concern or even mild derision. It must happen all the time. The bus, which arrives a moment later, completely ignoring a tangerine Plymouth facing the wrong way, in the middle of the road, is unlike any form of public transport I've ever seen.

It's an articulated hut for people, about fifty foot long with both ends higher than the middle – hence, I suppose, the local name for them – camels. With a belch of black smoke, the tractor unit hauls it away leaving us with the prospect of trying to reach Havana on three wheels.

No tyre is to be found, so I unload into another taxi, this time a slightly more modern '57 Chevy and, fingers crossed, proceed towards Havana.

Old Havana, close to the port and the sturdy Spanish colonial forts and palaces, is lively and picturesque and being slowly, carefully and beautifully restored. Which is a pity, as the mottled and peeling façades seem much closer to the spirit of this hot, steamy, hard-pressed city.

It's not difficult to pick up the Hemingway trail. Its epicentre is the Ambos Mundos Hotel, on the corner of Obispo and Mercaderes in the heart of the old city. On the wall are two plaques – one commemorating the frequent residence of Ernest H., who stayed here on numerous bachelor trips in the thirties, and the other dedicated to one George Washington Halsey who established the first daguerreotype photo studio in Cuba on this spot.

I'd never heard of him. Which must be the fate of many who share a wall with Ernest Miller Hemingway.

On the fifth floor of the Ambos Mundos Hotel is the room in which Hemingway reputedly began work on *For Whom the Bell Tolls* in 1939. (Michael Reynolds, one of his biographers, disputes this, saying that Hemingway was so famous by then that he used the Ambos Mundos as a public front, and actually double-booked a room in the Sevilla-Biltmore to give him space and peace for writing.)

Whatever the truth, I prefer to think that it was in Room 511 of the Ambos Mundos that Hemingway wrote the words that firmly established him in the post-coital lexicon by having Robert Jordan ask Maria, 'But did thee feel the earth move?' Maybe it's just because I'm a romantic and I'm right next door, in Room 509.

My good Cuban escort who is called Ernesto, but prefers the Beatles to bullfights, takes me to a small bar called the Bodeguita del Medio, on the grounds that it's old, established, traditional and noisy enough to anaesthetise jet lag.

The speciality of the house is *mojito* – a mix of rum, lime-juice, sugar, mint and ice – which is sharp and refreshing and agreeably addictive. There is a band playing in the tiny, breathless space, urging awkward foreigners into that state of constant rhythmic gyration that seems the natural state of most Cubans.

Fighting my way up to the bar, I'm rewarded not just by finding *chicharrones* – the best pork scratchings this side of Huddersfield – but also an endorsement of this establishment by one of the great barflies of our century. There, above the bottles, is written, in the now familiar curly script: 'My mojito in La Bodeguita, my daiquiri in El Floridita. Ernest Hemingway.'

Less eminent literary tributes are scrawled over every spare inch of the interior, including the bar and the bar stools. Someone has even managed to reach a seemingly inaccessible position twenty feet up on the wall, only to leave the frankly disappointing contribution, 'Geoff, You Fat Bastard.'

Later, in a Biblical upper room above the bar, its open balcony tempting in the faintest trace of a breeze, I sample my first Cuban meal. The roast pork is hardly exotic but the deep fried slices they call smashed bananas, the crispy sweet potatoes and a combination of black beans and rice known as *moriscos* – Moors and Christians – are unfamiliar, and very acceptable.

By the time I return to Room 509 at the Ambos Mundos, I have quite forgotten how I got here and where it was that my journey began twenty-three hours ago. Pretty soon, I can hear the trumpets of the bullfight, high-pitched laughter, and the clatter of typewriter keys from the room next door.

I'm into my first Cuban dream.

As I fumble for my room key a woman with long legs and golden hair passes by and goes into Hemingway's room. Even beyond the grave, his sexual magnetism hasn't deserted him.

Later, after a thin breakfast, but a great view, on the roof of the hotel, I realise that I too can visit Hemingway's room, for two dollars.

There isn't a lot there. Esperanza, the woman with long legs and golden hair who looks after the room, points out the bed in its alcove. It isn't actually *the* bed, but the Art Deco lamp-shade above it is *the* lampshade beneath which Hemingway lay – and which he must have seen flying around the ceiling after many a night out.

In the centre of the room is an ancient Royal typewriter, entombed beneath a Perspex cover like the relic of some long-dead saint. Esperanza's high heels click across the cool, tiled floor as she goes to the window and pulls it open, admitting a suffocating fug of warm, stale air and revealing The Famous View.

'The rooms on the north-east corner of the Ambos Mundos Hotel in Havana', wrote Hemingway in *Esquire* in 1933:

> ... *look out, to the north, over the old cathedral* [they still do], *the entrance to the harbour* [yes], *and the sea* [not quite, an ugly modern block with yellow plastic water tanks has gone up since then], *and to the east to Casablanca peninsula, the roofs of all houses in between and the width of the harbour.* [With its long

line of Spanish fortifications, that view can't have changed much since the beginning of the seventeenth century.] *If you sleep with your feet toward the east ... the sun, coming up over the Casablanca side and into your open window will shine on your face and wake you no matter where you were the night before.*

That's one thing I admire about Hemingway, he was never a hangover bore. He never let the night before spoil his enjoyment of the morning after.

Esperanza closes the window of Room 511 and apologises for the lack of memorabilia. His size 11 boots, some of his coats and a pair of his spectacles were here once but the people from the Hemingway museum at San Francisco de Paula took them away.

The village of San Francisco de Paula stands on a hill nine miles south of the city. It is not one of the smart suburbs of Havana, but then the Ambos Mundos was not one of Havana's smartest hotels.

As Hemingway got older, he may have enjoyed the kudos of being wined and dined by those who lived in commodious villas but, as a writer, his inclination was to live closer to the common people.

The approach to the gates of his house, Finca Vigía ('Lookout Farm') is off a rowdy main road whose bars, including El Brillante, once patronised by Hemingway, are now hard and basic drinking sheds. The short street that leads to the Finca is lined on both sides with modest wooden houses and cannot have changed much since Hemingway's time. The front of one of these houses has literally just fallen apart and as I walk by quite a crowd has gathered.

Everyone is out helping to prop it up and there is a lot of

noise and debate and gesturing and making of helpful suggestions and general good humour and I think I can see why Hemingway would have preferred the street life of San Francisco de Paula to dinner parties in smart Miramar.

The house, which his third wife Martha Gellhorn found through the small ads in 1939, was left to the Cuban government by Hemingway when he decided to leave his adopted island following Castro's revolution twenty years later.

It is looked after with meticulous care. Every object is noted and catalogued and located, as far as possible, in the same place it had when the Hemingways left. Nine thousand of his books remain on the shelves, each one hand-cleaned by the loyal staff. The public is allowed only as far as the doors and windows, which are thrown open but roped off.

Hemingway's ghost is in a mischievous mood today. In order to set up our filming, a small number of us are allowed over the cordon and into the precious interior. We fall silent. So perfect is the feat of preservation that it conveys the eerie impression that the Hemingways might have left the room only five minutes earlier. I stare at the armchair with its most un-macho pattern of leaves and blossoms and try to shift my imagination back forty years and put Hem in there and me opposite watching him pour a huge Gordon's gin from the tray that is still there with all his bottles on it, when my reverie is abruptly broken by a clatter, followed by a sharp intake of breath. Our thorough, careful, utterly mortified director has dislodged a piece of Venetian pottery from its precarious stand and it now lies in several pieces on the floor. Shock, horror, apology. We expect to be sent home immediately.

The curator gives a stern lecture, mercifully tempered by his admission that this particular piece has been broken once before. By Raisa Gorbachev. Our director, now a member of one of the most exclusive clubs in the world, feels a little better.

Hemingway's love of animals, dead or alive, permeates the house, from the stuffed heads of impala and kudu projecting from the dining room wall to lion skulls from Africa, pickled lizards in the bathroom and books on cats and cat care beside the bed. There were as many as fifty-seven cats living at the Finca, all of them given names with an 's' or a 'z' in – Crazy, Christian, Ecstasy, Funhouse, Fats, Friendless. Hemingway had a theory that this enabled them to hear their name called more easily.

Boise, the most spoiled cat of them all, was, as far as I can tell, the only living creature Hemingway ever allowed in the room when he was writing, apart from his beloved Black Dog.

My favourite room in the Finca is the bathroom next to his study. It has the best view in the house, a panorama of Havana with the sea in the distance, which can best be enjoyed from the lavatory seat. It also has a bat preserved in a bottle of formalin and a set of manually operated scales, alongside which is a most revealing and intimate glimpse of the man – a chart of his weight, inscribed in pencil on the wall, together with scribbled comments of explanation: '17 days off diet, 5 drinking', 203 lb, 'after Chinese dinner' and against one entry 'with slippers on and pyjamas'.

By now tour buses are filling the driveway and groups of Dutch, Germans and Italians are circling the house. We slip away through the gardens, to film on *Pilar*, the forty-foot boat which Hemingway bought in 1934 and gave in his will to his boatman Gregorio Fuentes. Fuentes, still alive at 101, gave the boat to the government who decided it should be preserved up here at the house. It's set, rather gloomily, in a concrete base with a massive timber cover, surrounded on three sides by swaying bamboo.

Filming in it isn't easy. I'm treated rather as we might treat a Cuban who wanted to roller-skate in Westminster Abbey.

They are clearly worried about letting me on deck at all, but eventually agree to my climbing aboard, provided I take my shoes off. When I make to sit on the fishing chair, shrieks of horror go up and I have to abort the attempt in mid-squat. It's a little sad to see this sturdy, practical, unflashy, walnut-hulled working boat ending her days as an untouchable object on a hill nine miles from the sea, but I suppose that's the price of fame.

Every night my bed at the hotel has a hand towel sculpture on it and a message from the girls who look after my room. Yesterday the towel had been ingeniously twisted into the shape of a bow tie, with a sheet of loo paper forming the knot in the middle. Tonight it's a heart, and the message beside it reads:

'Sr Michael, have a nice night. Your maids, Lilian and Isis.'

Having a nice night in old Havana can be interpreted many different ways. This is not a city for going to bed early with a good book. The streets are alive with all manner of temptations, most of them announced with the Havana hiss. This short sharp sibilance is quite normal amongst the locals but when directed at tourists it can mean an offer of anything from a guide or a Castro coin, to a cigar or a woman. I don't smoke and I've never seen the attractions of numismatics, so I'm left horribly vulnerable.

One of the odd things about Cuba is that, although only ninety miles away from the US coast, the island exists in a virtual news limbo.

Some of the hotels have CNN but I could find no foreign language magazines or newspapers on sale. There is one Cuban paper and it is called *Granma*. This eccentric title refers to the cabin cruiser *Granma* which brought Castro and Che Guevara back from exile in December 1956 to begin the struggle against the Batista government which led to its overthrow in 1959.

Granma is sold by all sorts of people, including the man who accosts me outside my hotel with what is probably the world's worst sales pitch.

'*Granma*?'

'No, thank you.'

'Well, fuck off then.'

Irresistible.

It's 33 degrees and heading higher. The humidity must be nudging 100. Wandering the streets isn't such a good idea and I am relieved that our film schedule is taking us indoors to the Corona cigar factory. Relief is short-lived. Though the small tourist shop where the credit cards are exchanged for elegantly wrapped boxes of cigars is air-conditioned, the huge factory behind it isn't. As the factory is far more interesting than the shop there seems no getting away from the stickiness.

I once visited the production line for a range of 'hand-finished' chocolates produced for a world-famous London department store. The 'hand-finishing' process consisted of a pair of elderly ladies waiting for the items to emerge from a coating machine, then dipping their gnarled forefingers into a bowl of melted chocolate and anointing each one with a twirl. What they did with their fingers in between each one was not always clear.

There are those who believe that the thighs of Cuban virgins are an integral part of cigar production, but in the long open room where 250 workers sit in rows at their workbenches there was no evidence of any below-the-belt work, and very few virgins.

At one end of the room is a stage with microphones set at a table and a large, badly reproduced photo of Che Guevara on an easel to one side. He is, of course, sporting a big cigar.

Occasionally there are readings to encourage the workers. Whilst we are there a lady exhorts them to higher cigar production with a passage from *The Old Man and the Sea.*

The workers are comparatively well paid. If you can roll more than 170 cigars in a working day you can earn 300 pesos a fortnight. That's about twelve pounds, or nineteen dollars. By comparison, a doctor or similar government employee would take almost a month to earn this much.

The irony is that the cigars which communist Cuba produces are one of the symbols of unrestrained capitalism, and there are those who would pay a hundred dollars or more for a hand-rolled Havana cigar. Which is about two and a half months' wages for the hand that rolled it. Or five months' wages for the teacher of their children.

Still very hot and today the wind has shifted to the east, blowing a sulphurous stench across the city from a chemical works down by the docks.

As usual, no sooner have we stepped outside the hotel than heads turn our way and people sidle across offering us everything. Basil's christened it Vampire City but in my experience this happens in the vicinity of any tourist hotel where there are rich people in a poor country. Two streets away you will be totally ignored.

Today the *Granma* salesman who told me to fuck off is full of good cheer as he has with him *Granma International* – English edition.

I fork out 50 cents for a copy and scan it as I walk down a narrow street incongruously called O'Reilly. I read of Cuba's record tourist figures, with Canadians and Italians leading the way, ahead of Germans and Spaniards. When Hemingway first walked these streets in the 1930s, Cuba was virtually another state of the USA, with its stranglehold on sugar, fruit canning and organised crime. All that changed with the Castro revolution, secured and bankrolled as it was by the Soviet Union. In the early 1960s Cuba abruptly became off-limits to Americans, a volatile flashpoint, the country most likely to spark off the third world war (though the US, inexplicably, held on to their naval base at Guantánamo).

Now the Russians have packed up and left and Castro is more interested in co-operation than confrontation. There are over 340 separate joint-venture projects and this week alone Mexican, Guatemalan, Norwegian and Spanish trade missions are in town.

The US government is not so keen to make up. It is not being allowed to by those Cubans who fled to America when their land was confiscated without compensation by Castro. They wait and watch from the comfort of nearby Florida and insist the pressure be kept on. Congress obliges them by maintaining a trade embargo. The Helms-Burton Act not only forbids American companies from carrying on trade with Cuba, but seeks to penalise non-American companies as well.

Meanwhile the locals still drive around in pre-Revolution American cars, Castro allows the dollar to be traded, the Afro-Cuban All Stars band wins a Grammy award and an American novelist remains one of Cuba's biggest tourist attractions. Crazy.

Hemingway's presence is never very far away. Fifteen minutes' walk from the Ambos Mundos – or three or four days if you stop to talk – there stands, beneath a fine old sign of swirling neon, his favourite Havana bar, El Floridita. It's little changed from the days when he would be snapped at the bar with Errol Flynn or Gary Cooper. Hemingway drank there a lot and drank a lot there.

Though I'm not allowed to sit in the hallowed corner which was, and still is, reserved for Hemingway, I'm as near as I can get to the altar, and I can see why he liked to sit here, back to the wall with a good all-round view. But then, Hemingway didn't just sit. He presided.

I can also understand why, as a connoisseur of the cocktail, he always preferred a seat at the bar to a seat at the table. From here I can follow every tip, twist, shake and stir of the mixing process.

In *Islands in the Stream*, he pulls off his old trick of selling self-destruction as exquisitely seductive:

Thomas Hudson had been ashore about four days when he got really drunk. It had started at noon at the Floridita ... He had drunk double frozen daiquiris, the great ones that Constante made, that had no taste of alcohol and felt, as you drank them, the way downhill glacier skiing feels running through powder snow and, after the sixth and eighth, felt like downhill glacier skiing feels when you're running unroped.

Never having experienced the thrills of downhill glacier skiing, roped or unroped, I sit myself down and order Hemingway's legacy to the Floridita, a variation of the daiquiri now known as the *Papa Doble* (lime-juice, dash of maraschino, double rum, *no* sugar, over crushed ice). Pretty soon, if not skiing, I'm certainly going downhill.

After my third *Papa Doble* I don't even care about the regular parade of tour groups, forty or fifty strong, who are herded into the Floridita to take photographs, buy nothing and leave. After four *Papa Dobles*, I've ceased to weep at the sight of Hemingway T-shirts and baseball caps piled up at the other end of the bar and, after five, I can even smile sweetly at the persistent irritation of the man who wants me to get the hell out of my seat so he can take a picture of his girlfriend on it.

All in all, I think Papa would have been proud of me. Except for the fact that I've only managed five of his specials.

His average was twelve at a sitting.

Still, it is only lunch-time.

Hemingway once called drink 'my best friend and severest critic'. I know what he means. This afternoon the daiquiris are my friends, making the blotchy, mouldering walls of old Havana glow with health, making the street life with all its complicated system of looks and glances and smiles and beckonings no longer aggressive and oppressive and claustrophobic but dramatic and endlessly entertaining. This is not a city for the inhibited. If you just let it flow over you, Havana is truly intoxicating.

The notes I made yesterday seem to stop in mid-afternoon, after three failed attempts to spell the word 'intoxicating'. The phone rings. Louder than usual, I swear. It's my producer, Martha. We have secured an interview with Gregorio Fuentes, Hemingway's 101-year-old skipper of the *Pilar*. He lives at Cojímar a few miles along the coast, and can see us at eleven thirty.

Wash and shave and reach for the towel. It's been wound in the shape of a swan. Take a while to undo it.

My head is a bit sore – inside rather than outside – and before setting off for Cojímar, I cross the street to find something to soothe it at Johnson's, a venerable chemist's shop whose scantily laden shelves and old wooden galleries stretch off into the depths of a cool and mercifully dark interior. I explain my malady to one of the staff who disappears into the gloom leaving me to contemplate a display-case full of dusty condom packets.

There is a passage in *Islands in the Stream* in which Thomas Hudson, after several too many at the Floridita, struggles to find a Seconal capsule with which to head off a hangover. (He knocks it off his bedside table and it's eventually found by his cat.) It sounds so like an autobiographical detail that I ask the lady who brings back my preparation if Hemingway ever came in here on his merry way up the street from hotel to bar. There is some mirth as this is translated and they nod and giggle and tell me he always used to come in here for his PPG 5. Thinking I have a scoop, I write this information down with laborious care. This only seems to increase their amusement, and it's not until later in the day that I learn that PPG 5 has only been on the market for five years, and though its primary purpose is to reduce cholesterol it's been found to have distinctly Viagran side effects. All of which would have suited Papa admirably. If only he'd been alive.

The soggy clouds have departed and it is a roaring furnace of a day as we approach Cojímar. Grey concrete-slab blocks loom to the south but the shoreline of the little bay is still dominated by the graceful Spanish fortress at its mouth and the stone jetty that snakes into the water beside it. It doesn't look to have changed much since the days when Hemingway kept *Pilar* in the harbour and chose the local fishing community as the setting for his most successful book *The Old Man and the Sea*. They have returned the compliment by raising a memorial to him, a small colonnaded shrine which circles a bronze head of Hemingway, made from melted brass off local fishing boats. It just misses looking like the man. From one side it's George V, from the other, Lenin.

The Terraza, the waterside watering hole that Hemingway frequented, still flourishes, and it's here that Gregorio will talk to us.

It has a long polished-wood bar and at the back, overlooking the sea, is a smart restaurant with photographs of Gregorio and Ernest hauling in various sizes of marlin sharing the wall with an interestingly mis-spelled pottery dish on which is engraved a recipe for 'Ceviche à la Himisngway,' a traditional fish stew.

As we are looking for a good filming position, a dark shadow blots out the sunlight. It is cast by an enormous double-decker tourist coach which has drawn up outside and which disgorges an obedient crocodile of tourists all heading for the room in which we are hoping to talk to Gregorio. There has been a double-booking between ourselves and fifty Belgians, and the manager makes his preference quite clear.

Gregorio and his grandson and minder, Rafaelito, sportingly agree to relocate the meeting at a boat-yard down by the shore, where the Cojímar River runs into the bay. Tourists don't come down here, certainly not in groups of forty or fifty, and it's rather peaceful and local. By the bridge, a father is teaching his small son to fish with a hand-line and families cluster round a hut drinking *guarapo*, an iced sugar-cane drink, out of brown glass tumblers. Nearby stalls sell staple snacks – fried bananas, sweet corn, toasted bread. An old man studies the sky, critically, through a pair of old binoculars. It looks perfect to me, but he doesn't seem happy. (We didn't know then that Hurricane George, one of the fiercest of the season, was slowly gaining strength in the eastern Caribbean.)

In the yard the local fishing boats, which sport endearing names like *Gladys* and *Doris*, are being painted and repaired, mostly without the aid of modern technology. Handsaws cut timbers, rivets are driven home by hand. Into the midst of all this, sitting in a 1957 Hillman Minx driven by Rafaelito, comes Gregorio Fuentes, the longest-surviving of all Hemingway's old pals, a man who has spent eighty years of his life in boats and is now one of the most famous fishermen since St Peter.

He is simply, smartly turned out in grey trousers and a crisp, clean shirt with a green stripe. He sports a dark blue cap with the words 'Capitán Gregorio Fuentes' unnecessarily printed across it. He is tall and stoops only slightly and carries a crutch but seems not to depend on it. He smokes a cigar with obvious relish and when he shakes all our hands, I notice he holds on to Martha's much longer than anyone else's.

A hundred and one? I'd like to be that active at sixty.

Rafaelito has given me certain guidelines about the interview. I should 'avoid philosophicals' – and he'll not answer questions involving drinking habits or female relationships. This, of course, suggests there is a lot to ask. He fills me in quickly on things I ought to know. They were good friends, Hemingway and Gregorio; Hemingway came to the house. It was not a boss–worker relationship. It was a relationship of mutual respect.

Gregorio is a little tired, Rafaelito goes on, there was a South African crew talking to him yesterday and some Indians are expected tomorrow. In addition people keep dropping in to see him at the house (paying fifty dollars for fifteen minutes). The old man, he says, is 'a living museum'. And clearly doing a lot better business than most museums.

By now Gregorio is seated and impatient to begin. As soon as I put the first question, hammering starts somewhere in the yard and we have to wait until Martha has located and placated the source.

Despite the midday heat Gregorio replies to my questions with the patience of a saint. He looks like one for a start. With his long craggy face and big tired eyes he resembles the victim in a medieval temptation painting.

He tells how Hemingway came across him whilst both were fishing in Key West and how he had told him he was having a boat built and wanted Gregorio to come and be her skipper. Hemingway was a man, he assures me, 'who had a human heart for everybody, especially kids and poor people'.

He was with Hemingway when they came across the lone fisherman who became the inspiration for Hemingway's best-known story.

'I suggested to title the book *The Old Man and the Sea*,' he adds modestly.

Despite the warning, I feel I can't completely avoid the forbidden areas, but I phrase my question carefully.

'I read somewhere that Hemingway never drank whilst fishing ...?'

Gregorio replies without a pause. 'No! He always drank.' Then his eyes fix on me. And his eyes are quite something. Though the rest of his expression may seem tired and detached, his eyes are big and full of life. They give away what he's really thinking and I think it is that I'm a bit tiresome.

'Many people saw him with a drink in his hand and they thought he was always drunk, but go to hell, they didn't know what they were talking about.'

'Which of his wives was the best fisherwoman?'

'None of them.'

'What do you think of the American blockade of Cuba? D'you think that will change soon?'

Gregorio removes his cigar, but the smoke lingers a long time around his mouth.

'I heard Hemingway once say that there was going to be a big war and the whole world was going to defeat the United States and leave them even less powerful than a small island like Cuba.'

'Do you believe this?'

'Yes, I think so.'

By the time we've finished both myself and Ernesto, who has been making a brilliant instant translation, are exhausted. Gregorio looks fresh as a daisy. For the first time in half an hour I take my eyes off his and look around. All work in the boat-yard has ceased and behind the camera, a crowd of local fishermen has downed tools to stand and watch the local hero.

*

Havana is full of music and musicians, especially after dark. Not just in clubs but in the streets and in the bars and in the restaurants. There is no hiding from them. The bands will seek you out, wherever you are. Tea for two can easily become tea for twelve. No nook or cranny, back room or dimly lit alcove is safe from a few choruses of 'Guantanamera'. The lobby of the Ambos Mundos Hotel is no exception. Every evening a portly tenor and his even more portly accompanist thunder out their operatic repertoire as the life of a busy hotel lobby goes on around them.

This evening is particularly busy and the only table we can find is next door to the lavatory. A big middle-aged Cuban lady sits patiently on a chair outside and occasionally acts as a guide to very drunk tourists who can't find the entrance. She also has to go and look for them when they don't come out. We all like her, but Basil has taken a particular shine and tonight she confides to him that she was once a pretty fair opera singer herself.

Encouraged by us all, she waits until the portly tenor has crescendoed yet again, and as he mops his brow and looks swiftly round for any response, she rises from her seat, draws herself up to an impressive height and silences the lobby with a heartbreaking Spanish love-song. Leaving not a dry eye in the house she graciously acknowledges the thunderous applause and resumes her seat beside the lavatory.

Later, we eat at a *paladar*. Owing to a serious shortage of restaurants, the authorities have licensed an arrangement whereby families can charge for providing meals in their homes, as long as they are limited to twelve chairs and staffed only by members of the family. It's an odd sensation to be giving our order to the waitress at one end of the room, whilst her grandfather and two children are watching television at the other. Our menu has an English translation and includes Hot Entrances and Cream Soap.

When someone said that I should not leave Havana without seeing Marina Hemingway, I scuttled back to my books to see if there was a sister I'd missed. Or perhaps a secret daughter no one talked about.

But the search for Marina Hemingway doesn't lead to any undiscovered relatives or skeleton-filled closets. It leads along the Malecón, the crusty peeling crescent of seafront, through a tunnel and out past the green-lawned villas of Miramar, which is the nearest thing to a Beverly Hills in Havana, over a creek at Jaimanitas, where run-down fishing-boats are huddled at crazy angles on the shore, and through a security gate, above which flutters a Cuban flag.

This is Marina Hemingway. One of the most ambitious waterfront developments in Cuba. An international 'sports port' as they call it, themed, relentlessly, after the most famous non-Cuban of them all.

You can take one of the 186 rooms at 'The Old Man and the Sea' Hotel, or one of the 314 rooms at 'The Garden of Eden'. You can wander down to Wild Ernie's for a drink, stuff yourself at 'The Green Hills of Africa' and sweat it all off in Papa's Solarium.

I drive past these various temptations until I reach the waterfront. Out there beyond the harbour mouth is what, more than anything else, drew Hemingway to Cuba. La Corriente, the Gulf Stream. A sixty-mile-wide, mile-deep fisherman's paradise.

This Gulf Stream you are living with, knowing, learning about, and loving, has moved, as it moves, since before man, and that it has gone by the shoreline of that long, beautiful, unhappy island since before Columbus sighted it ... That stream will flow, as it has flowed, after the Indians, after the Spaniards, after the British, after the Americans and after all the Cubans and all the systems of governments, the richness, the poverty, the martyrdom, the sacrifice and the venality and the cruelty are all gone.

Hemingway's long rap in *Green Hills of Africa* is not all celebration. Like the good reporter he once was, he notes, with equal relish, the 'high-piled scow of garbage' which the tugboats of Havana dump into the deep blue waters, 'the flotsam of palm fronds, corks, bottles, and used electric light globes, seasoned with an occasional condom or a deep-floating corset, the torn leaves of a student's exercise book, a well-inflated dog, the occasional rat, the no-longer-distinguished cat'.

Nevertheless, Hemingway elevated marlin-fishing on the Gulf Stream into one of life's last great adventures. He went at it day after day after day, so much so that local fishermen christened the stretch of water east from Cojímar 'Hemingway's Mile'. And when he wasn't fishing it he was writing about it and even working with scientists from the Smithsonian to classify the various marlin species. It was a very serious obsession.

In 1950, never really happy with any activity unless some sort of contest was involved, Hemingway started an International Marlin Tournament. Ten years later the competition was named after him, though he resisted this – 'A lousy posthumous tribute to a lousy living writer' – and the first prize that year was won by Fidel Castro.

One of this year's main fishing tournaments has been running for two days and has two more to go. There is only one Cuban boat in the competition, a couple of Canadians, and the rest, surprisingly, are American. The Cuban organisers are helpful and suggest we wait until the boats come in and ask if any would be happy to take us aboard tomorrow morning.

At six, the boats start to come back in and the lucky ones can be picked out long before they dock by the number of white pennants they have run up. One for each catch.

I notice straightaway that there has been a major change since Hemingway fished here. This is the age of tag and release. Not only is it not necessary to kill the marlin to score points, you actually get fewer points if you do kill one.

So there are plenty of pennants but no one hoisting dead marlin up on the weighing post and posing for a photo as Ernie loved to do.

I approach an American boat with two fluttering white pennants and introduce myself.

'I'm from the BBC.'

Instant recognition. 'Ah yes!' says the skipper, shaking my hand warmly. 'The Bahamas Billfish Championship.'

In the world of deep-sea fishing, the BBC means only one thing.

They're a friendly crew and lead the competition after two days. They're happy to play host to us tomorrow, but they warn us to be on time. The starting gun goes off at nine sharp.

The starting gun is not quite as impressive as it sounds. It's a small brass cannon, carried from the clubhouse to the shore in the back of a car and set up at a point opposite which the sixteen competing boats are lined up.

With due ceremony, the breech is filled with rifle powder and the barrel stuffed with sheet after sheet of toilet paper, laboriously folded, inserted and rammed home with a plunger.

On the stroke of nine o'clock a match is applied and the rifle powder and the toilet paper combine to raise a respectable thump, which sends the cannon reeling back and the boats gunning their engines and racing off toward the waiting marlin.

This is quite a thrill. To be about to hit what Hemingway called 'the great blue river'. Conditions are good as our wooden-hulled 55-footer slaps and bounces on a lively sea.

About three miles out from the shore, perhaps a little less, the colour of the water indeed changes very abruptly, from milky green to a blue, more royal than navy, with lines of wind-spun silver foam slanting through it.

Our hosts are five Americans out of West Palm Beach. I ask them why the majority of boats in the tournament are from the USA when that country forbids trade with Cuba.

They come, they say, because this is the best marlin-fishing in the world, and for this they are prepared to accept certain restrictions. All supplies, right down to bread and water, must be brought with them from the States. They are not allowed to buy anything Cuban, nor are they allowed to accept anything from the Cubans by way of prize money or on-shore hospitality. American customs pay them a lot of attention when they return to Florida.

The organisers have issued a map of the fishing zone, divided into alphabetical squares. Square F is the best. It is where the coastline juts out to meet the stream and the marlin are most likely to stop and feed. It's also right at the mouth of the harbour, opposite the old city, visible once upon a time from Room 511 at the Ambos Mundos.

It's also the busiest and our skipper, up on the flying bridge, decides to head a little further north and east before putting out the lines.

Four rods are fished, but apart from one false alarm, there is a lot of watching, waiting and application of sun cream. Little else. Explanatory theories are concocted – the wind has slipped away from due east, the most favourable direction. There's too much direct sunlight. The middle of the day is always the worst time. No one mentions the Palin effect.

The sun climbs, hangs and begins to fall. The skipper puts the boat about and we begin to readjust our position a little nervously. But still nothing breaks the waters.

At the end of the day's fishing, at six o'clock, we return to shore empty-rodded, hoping everyone else will have done so too. But there have been strikes and other people's flags are flying and one boat is still out there. A huge marlin was hooked early on this morning by one of the women in her crew and she has held on to it all day long and is prepared to hang on all night if necessary.

Now that is hard to take. A Hemingway adventure is happening out there and we have no way of getting to it.

Our crew is still optimistic. They were unlucky today, but their first two days' tally keeps them up with the leaders and in with a chance. They've invited us to return tomorrow, the last day of the tournament.

A nxious to sample all the myriad forms of Cuban transport, I ride out to the Marina today in a motorcycle sidecar. They were very popular in Sheffield when I was a lad, but they tend to be consigned to transport museums nowadays.

Cuba is a living transport museum, so you still see plenty of them, jostling for road space with Chevy Bel Airs from the 1950s, stretch Skodas from the 1960s, horse-drawn buggies from the 1740s, and lots of bicycles and scooters of indeterminate age, often with *parilleras* aboard. *Parilleras* are the girls who sit sideways on the back of bicycles, usually wearing eye-catching fluorescent Lycra shorts. My driver points to them as we speed along the Avenida Zoologico, and expresses a warm enthusiasm.

'Especially the ones with big bottoms!' he yells into the slipstream. A sign of beauty in Cuba, evidently.

Aboard ship and out onto the famous blue water. Except that it isn't so blue today. The wind has turned again and slabs of iron-grey cloud loom over us, blotting out the sun and washing out the colours of yesterday. The competition ends at two o'clock and by then our boat has not even a false alarm to show for its last days' sailing. Very sportingly, they allow me on the fishing chair for the last few hours of daylight. And, of course, everyone hopes that beginner's luck might yet save the day.

The swell heaves and sighs and I learn how to let my line out and how to control the reel and I grow mesmerised by the dot of colour that is my float, bobbing on the water, and desperate to feel some sort of pull on it. My instructor tells me exactly what to do in the event of a huge marlin impaling itself on the end of my line. Pump and reel, pump and reel.

But the light begins to go and there's still no one down there in the marlin department. We head back to the Marina for the last time. For all his action writing, Hemingway understood failure pretty well. I re-read the opening lines of *The Old Man and the Sea*, and don't feel so bad.

He was an old man who fished alone in a skiff in the Gulf Stream and he had gone eighty four days now without taking a fish.

Our American crew has been kind and generous with us. There's little we can do but bid them farewell and promise to change our name to Albatross Productions.

Thunder rumbles and lightning flashes out over the sea as we ride home.

Any lingering dejection is dispersed by the hero's welcome I receive back at the hotel. Thrusting a copy of *Granma* into my hand, Isis and Lilian gaze at me with new respect. 'There, Mr Michael, in the television listings!'

I look for the column. There are only four pages in today's issue so it's not hard to find.

'*Criaturas Feroces,*' I read, 'con Jamie Lee Curtis y Michael Palin.'

My stock has soared. I'm no longer a common or garden Hemingway fan. I'm Jamie Lee Curtis's co-star.

And the towel on my bed tonight is in the shape of the letter 'M'.

Heavy rain in the night and, as I push open the windows of my room next to Hemingway's, the roofs are steaming, and Hurricane George is creeping slowly towards us. With a bit of luck we'll be out in time. George is moving out of Puerto Rico and heading for Dominica. Tomorrow we leave Cuba for the States to cover the last few Hemingway destinations.

Take a last walk around some of my favourite places. Like the Plaza de Armas, surrounded by fine colonial edifices, the most impressive of which is the grandly named Palace of The Captains General, now the City Museum. A tremendous colonnade of grey limestone walls and pillars, as massive and serious as anything in classical Europe.

The communists have been surprisingly generous with the monuments of imperialism, and the rooms of the museum are an eloquent evocation of the days when the colonialists lived well in Havana. The rooms are unbearably hot, and yet the be-wigged and overcoated grandees in the portraits appear to be dressed for a funeral in Greenland. Is this yet more evidence of global warming or did people still dress up for their portraits in those days?

For our last meal in Havana we go to the tiny Chinatown area to see if Hemingway's favourite Chinese restaurant, El Pacifico, is still there. And it is, a monumental barn of a place, occupying several floors of a building in a narrow street in the Cayo Hueso area. They say that in the old days the restaurant occupied the ground floor and the floors above were arranged in ascending order of decadence – first: gambling, second: sex, and third: drugs. The penthouse presumably offered gambling, sex *and* drugs, and possibly donkeys as well.

There is no trace of dissipation in the darkened entrance where an unimpressive menu is advertised and no one on the staff seems to know or care if Hemingway used to bring his family here for Sunday lunch.

So we go across the road and eat our meal in the small back room of another Chinese establishment – not too small, however, for a six-piece band to squeeze in and supply 'Guantanamera' with the steamed rice.

A last round of *mojitos* at the Patio restaurant in the fine old Cathedral Square. Normally at this time the place is ringed with professional ladies weighing up business prospects, but tonight I'm told there has been one of the periodic police crackdowns and only the real die-hards are left.

To the airport in a vintage Chrysler. As it is precisely the same age as the black Chrysler that Hemingway used to drive, there is always a chance he swung this one round the same corners. Not always with much success.

In a letter to Maxwell Perkins from the Finca in July 1945, Hemingway describes yet another messy accident, '[It] was at noon and I was cold sober,' before adding, more incriminatingly, 'Fourth bad smash in a year. Fortunately only two got into print.'

Amazingly enough, in 1955, the most accident-prone man in the world was awarded the Order of St Christopher, for those who had driven exceptionally safely in Havana. Hemingway apparently regarded this as more precious than the Nobel Prize he'd won the year before. He passed the Nobel medal on to a church at Cobre near Santiago de Cuba. And there it resides to this day, in the Chapel of Our Lady of Miracles.

This seems typical of Hemingway's life here. The bold, if eccentric, gesture of a man who knew that in Cuba, bold eccentric gestures were much appreciated in a man, along with any show of confident flamboyance. Hemingway hated limitation and constriction of any kind, especially social and cultural. If he had lived and worked in America, he would have been required to conform in some way to the expectations of a literary establishment. In Cuba he didn't have to pay this price.

However, he had done himself lasting damage in the crashes in Africa, and, throughout the late fifties, his health, and the health of the island, declined rapidly. Castro's revolution in 1959 was seen by most Cubans as a cure. For Hemingway, it was equivalent to a terminal diagnosis.

As Castro and the USA began to square off, he was forced into an agony of divided loyalties between home and homeland. On 25 July 1960, he took the ferry to Key West and sailed away from Cuba for the last time.

Thirty-eight years on, there is no ferry to Key West or anywhere else on the US coast. The country of Hemingway's birth and the country he adopted are still squaring up, which is why I'm leaving Cuba on a Jamaican plane, heading *south* to the USA.

AMERICAN WEST

'This is a cockeyed wonderful country,' wrote Hemingway to his artist buddy Waldo Peirce, after two weeks in Wyoming in August 1928. Despite his close acquaintance with Italy, France and Spain, this was the first time the much-travelled twenty-nine-year-old had tasted the wide open spaces of his own country.

The birth of his second son two months previously had brought him back from Europe and the need to get away and finish his new novel (which became A Farewell to Arms) had sent him out to the American West in search of peace and quiet.

He returned many times to the Big Country on the eastern slopes of the Rockies. It was a safety valve, a place to hunt and shoot and fish and finish books and read proofs well away from the metropolitan literary environment he disliked so much.

He never made a home here, that is, until the winter of 1958, when he and Mary first rented and then bought a house on a hillside in Ketchum, Idaho. But by that time the West was no longer the place where he could get away from his problems. It was the place where his problems finally caught up with him.

In November 1930, when Archie MacLeish flew out to Montana to see his friend Ernest hospitalised in Billings after a serious car crash, it took him two days to get there and he called it 'the most hair raising flight of my life'.

My first trip to Montana is not much better. Huge thunderstorms in the Mid-West empty the clouds and fill the airports, and by the time we reach Bozeman there is snow on the ground and hardly a room to be had because of parents' weekend at the university.

I'm told that though Montana is the fourth largest state by area, it has a population of less than eight hundred thousand. This should make for wide open spaces, but tonight downtown Bozeman is like Times Square. The only difference is that they treat you better here. However hectic is the bar or the baggage-hall, no one but yourself is going to hurry you.

By the time I get to bed I haven't seen a single wide open space but already I feel a deep and inexplicable sense of relaxation.

When he and his friend Bill Horne first came out west in 1928, in a yellow Ford runabout provided for him by Pauline's ever-generous Uncle Gus, Hemingway found it hard to settle. Though he thought it 'damned lovely country', he couldn't find a dude ranch (a ranch that took paying guests) which suited him. The first one, Folly Ranch, had fifteen girls staying, which was not what he wanted at all (though Bill Horne married one of them). In another he found the peace and solitude too much, and once again confided in Waldo Peirce. 'Am lonely as a bastard, drank too much last night and feel like anything but work now.'

When he returned with Pauline two years later, they hit upon a ranch called the L-Bar-T on the eastern edge of Yellowstone National Park, just south of the old mining town of Cooke City, Montana. It was run by a Swede, Lawrence Nordquist, who offered them a cabin in the woods with a view of the mountains. Hemingway loved the fishing in the nearby Clarks Fork River and he and Pauline and the family returned to the Nordquist ranch throughout the thirties, until fame and another divorce lured Hemingway to the lusher pastures of Sun Valley, Idaho.

This morning, early, we load up and head south to see Yellowstone Park for ourselves. I can't match Hemingway's yellow Ford, but given the nature of the weather, have accepted the kind offer of a Ford F250, a big bruiser of a pick-up that, literally, weighs a ton.

The day looks promising, a big, largely clear sky with licks of grey cloud on the Bridger mountains to the north-east. At Livingston we swing south and follow the Yellowstone River, past turn-offs to places whose names tell you all the essentials of local history. Pray, Emigrant and Miner.

The valley road, bordered by pale and ghostly stands of silver birch is still dark, but the snow-covered slopes of the high mountains ahead of us shine gloriously in the first brightness of the rising sun. Highway 89 feels like the road to heaven.

Once we're inside the park boundaries, there's a dramatic change of scenery. A third of Yellowstone Park was burned by multiple fires in 1988 and we pass through a desolate and depressing landscape of slopes strewn with scorched and broken pine trees.

But where the grass grows there is plenty of life. A wolf, businesslike and preoccupied, trots off into the trees, a herd of elk passes more slowly, the females calling to each other in high-pitched whinnies. Every now and then the bull elk lets out a high, pumping cry which is known, accurately enough, as a bugle. A solitary bison with its huge head and spindly back legs grazes beside an old cavalry post. He looks vaguely incongruous, as if he's been put there by the tourist office, but once he and his kind had this land pretty much to themselves. Nearly two hundred years ago, when the explorers Lewis and Clark made the first overland crossing of America, they reported that it took them ten days to ride through one bison herd. There are now fewer than three thousand left in the three and a half thousand square miles of Yellowstone Park.

High point of the day's journey is the Craig Pass on the Continental Divide. Not only are we up above eight thousand feet but there's something about the name and the concept of a continental divide that has always appealed. Like the North or South Pole or the source of the Amazon, it's a place that is far more significant than it looks.

Spend a while turning my head one way and then the other, trying to take in the fact that rain falling on one side of me drains east to the Mississippi, and rain falling on the other side of me may well end up coming out of a lawn sprinkler in Beverly Hills. We return home past the thermal wonders of the Park like the Old Faithful Geyser and the bubbling Fountain Paint Pot hot springs. I toy with the idea of a documentary on such places called This Flatulent Earth.

But the big sights are full of people and that was what Hemingway came out west to get away from. He came to write and hunt and I must try and find some of his present-day counterparts.

Breakfast at Big Sky, an hour's ride from Bozeman up the dramatic Gallatin Valley, with rugged vertical rock faces on its east bank and a fast, bustling river. This is skiing country and the buildings are raised on stone pilings against the winter conditions.

This time of year, October, is, I'm told, about the best time to visit. Less busy than the summer, more accessible than the winter, and beautiful too, with the sun hitting at dramatically low angles.

Hemingway enjoyed driving across America. In his sixtieth year, he drove through Iowa, Nebraska and Wyoming, keeping himself going, according to his biographer Carlos Baker, by listening to the World Series and 'stopping at grocery stores in the smaller towns to buy apples, cheese, and pickles, which he washed down with Scotch and fresh lime juice.' Eurghh.

At the side of the road just before Big Sky resort there is a long single-storey building with a log-cabin finish called the Corral Bar. It's a folksy, friendly place with a good smell of bacon and fresh coffee and, I like to think, just the sort of spot where Hemingway would have found the company he liked. The rest-rooms are called 'Bucks' and 'Does' and the decoration favours things like bleached deer skulls. A huge moose-head hangs out over one of the tables. It bears an expression of amused tolerance and the curly-haired bison next to it looks positively angelic. Man, beast and breakfast in perfect harmony.

The elk-shooting season begins today, and the bow-hunting season ends. I get talking to a group of hunters, all around thirty or forty, with very big moustaches, who are about to leave for three or four days of elk-hunting in the outback.

I tell them I've heard some pretty unpleasant stories of modern convenience hunters, would-be Hemingways who drive out to game farms and on payment of several thousand dollars, have a farm-raised moose or elk led out for them to shoot in a fenced-off area. Kill guaranteed. Maximum amount of money for the minimum of effort.

This group condemns such people vociferously. They're not hunters. All they want is a trophy. The real difference between the two approaches seems to boil down to the same answer I've had from everyone who hunts. Respect for the animal.

'I have more respect for elk than I do for most people,' one of them maintains, which just about sums up this curious commingling of sentiment and slaughter.

They regard the tracking as an essential part of hunting, and they describe the delights of stalking their prey over difficult terrain.

'You can find a nice fresh big bold track in snow, you know, fresh that morning and still steaming droppings, and you know you're right on him and he's walking five miles an hour and you're only going three. You have to run sometimes. It gets pretty exciting.'

They seem to enjoy the risks. They tell stories of being bitten in the thigh by grizzly bears and charged by buffalo, as if these were what made the whole thing worth while.

They believe it's important to make use of what they kill. One of them thinks that you should have to prove you're going to eat the animal before you're allowed to hunt it, which seems quite reasonable to me. Up here where winter lasts six months of the year, people need the meat and the livelihood that comes from hunting. Nothing of the elk they kill is wasted, even the antlers are sold to Korea for what they call, possibly euphemistically, vitamin supplement.

The other element is that of tradition. Though two or three of these hunters are old Californian hippies, they do regard the shouldering of the gun as tapping in to a great American tradition and an even greater universal tradition. As one puts it, they see themselves as part of 'the cycle of life in the mountains'.

An hour later, having tapped in to the Great American Breakfast, we start back to Bozeman. The hunting party has forded the white waters of the Gallatin River and is clambering slowly up the steep, snow-slippery hill on the far bank. I feel a nagging envy. I'd go with them like a shot if I didn't have to kill an elk.

Back at the motel, where meat we haven't killed is being prepared for our dinner, I pick up a copy of a local Sunday paper – the *Billings Gazette*. The ghost of Ernest flutters out of its pages. Inside the paper is a long feature on Dr Louis Allard, one of Billings' greatest medical men, and the doctor who operated on Hemingway's broken arm sixty-eight years ago, after the accident that brought Archie MacLeish out to Montana to see him. There is Ernest, arm in plaster and a big bandage around him, looking bashful and, as he tended to do when injured, a little pleased with himself.

Later, as I'm about to settle down to sleep, I hear a sound which conveys better than anything in nature the sense of these wide, wild spaces. It's the long, low wail of a passing freight train. As the mournful sound dies away, I pick up a collection of stories about Montana. It's called *The Last Best Place*.

L ike the hunters up at Big Sky, Hemingway had an odd respect for the animals whose lives he brought to an end with such regularity.

The more favoured of his victims ended up sharing his house with him. The walls of the Finca Vigia in Havana bristle with all manner of proud beasts. Buffalo, oryx and kudu in the bedroom, Grant's gazelle in the living-room, pronghorn in the dining-room, hartebeest in the hallway. In the library a leopard stares glassily up from the floor, snarl frozen on its handsome jaws, in the guest room two lion skulls occupy the shelf above Norman Mailer's *The Naked and the Dead*, a writing desk in the tower room rests firmly on a flattened lion.

Hemingway, by nature a reluctant spender, must have made an exception for taxidermists.

Stuffed heads and mounted skins seem to belong to the past, and I'm wondering if the modern hunter has the same inclination to hang his catches up on the wall. There is a taxidermist in a quiet suburb of Bozeman who I hope will be able to supply a few answers.

He lives and works from a house in a respectable development of modern, prairie-style houses called Outlaw Drive, which is off a road of equally respectable houses known as Wild Bunch Drive. To confuse matters even more, the suburb is called Belgrade.

There is no neon sign advertising Jerome Andres' business, and the casual visitor strolling down Outlaw Drive might easily be confused by what is going on at No. 2950. A deer lies dead on the front lawn, a skinned corpse hangs in the open garage, swinging gently above a sea of antlers, and a mighty half-mounted bison head guards the door of one of the outbuildings.

As I walk up the short driveway I pass scatterings of horn and skin, a circular saw and a large plastic bin of jawbones marked 'Inedible'.

Jerome Andres, the owner and proprietor, comes out to meet me, or to be more accurate I bump into him as he emerges carrying a moose-head from the workshop to the garage. He pulls the garage door a little wider and I can see quite grisly scenes of carnage in there.

He deposits his load in businesslike fashion and reappears. He's a short, powerfully built man in jeans and a neat blue check shirt with long, greying sideburns protruding from a baseball cap, which he raises every now and then to wipe his brow, revealing a balding pate. He hitches up his trousers, smiles a little shyly and motions me to the door from which he first emerged. I feel faint unease and am glad that the sun's shining and I'm not alone. In fact the door leads to a quite tasteful reception area. It is full of animals, but, unlike those in the garage, most of them are in one piece. There are a couple of heads in plastic bags nestling by the computer, but the room is a Noah's Ark-like showpiece for taxidermy. A sign above the reception desk defines his business philosophy: 'The Bitterness of Poor Quality remains long after the Sweetness of Low Price is Forgotten.'

The phone goes, Jerome deals with it quickly and sympathetically and as he replaces the receiver jots a name down on a pad.

'They're bringing a mountain goat in at noon.'

Jerome, or Jerry as he asks us to call him, is clearly a busy man. He was himself a hunter who learned taxidermy at eighteen and has taught it all over the States.

He takes us through in to the workshop. The smell is bad, a mixture of the sickly sweetness of flesh and blood and the pungency of epoxy resin and spray paint. He's currently working on a moose-head. In this confined space it looks enormous, like a small meteorite. He apologises for having to keep working as he talks and begins to brush the horns before spray-painting the nose and around the eyes with the care and delicacy of a make-up artist.

He takes pride in this part of the process and says, without apparent irony, 'Sometimes we make the animals better than they were before.'

In another room off the back of the workshop is the rest of Jerry's workforce. One man is carefully removing fur from a goat's legs, another is making a pair of eyes to fit an antelope skin stretched tight on a polystyrene mould.

'These will eventually pop out through the head,' he explains, helpfully.

A young woman with tumbling curly hair sits and paints another mould, another plaits what looks like bison beard. A radio plays quietly. The atmosphere is serene and studious. They could be embroidering a tapestry or illuminating manuscripts. Only the lingering fetid smell and a containerful of skinned heads gives it away.

Jerry is constantly being interrupted. Two men have just pulled into his driveway and are unloading a two-year-old pronghorn antelope. They're very sure how they want it mounted. Body sideways on, in relief, with the head turned as if it's looking out into the room.

Could Jerry do it by February? One of the men wants to give it as a present to his wife on Valentine's Day.

Jerry sizes it up, makes a measurement or two and there and then, right on the front lawn, produces a short, sharp knife and begins to remove the skin from the body. He asks one of the men to hold it down with his foot whilst, with a quick and expert twist, he breaks the head off. As he pulls it away the skin follows neatly, like a coat being slipped from a pair of shoulders.

He carries the flayed carcass to the dreaded garage. He'll clean the skin up tonight, remove all the flesh, turn the ears inside out, the lips will be split, salted and dried and then the skin will be sent to the local tannery.

'Will you have it stuffed by February?' I ask.

Jerry looks pained at the use of the 's' word.

'Stuffing is when you stuff something in a bag,' he says a trifle tartly. 'This is artistic improvement.'

'Will it be artistically improved by February?'

'Not a chance.'

The customer will have to wait over a year for his funny Valentine. Jerry has two hundred animals awaiting treatment, an African shipment is expected, there's a water-buffalo in his workshop and the elk season started yesterday. The taxidermy business has clearly survived Hemingway's death.

What I should like to do now is to gauge the health of another business that was once close to Hemingway's heart. His doorway to the West, the dude ranch. The L-Bar-T no longer takes guests but plenty of others do, and the brochures compete fiercely in offering temptations for jaded city folk.

My favourite selling claim is the ranch that boasts, 'Our view is out of sight!'

That should be worth not seeing.

Kalispell, Montana, is 275 miles, as the eagle flies, to the north-west of Bozeman, just to the far side of the Flathead Mountains, where the Rockies spread towards the Canadian border.

I'm waiting at the airport for my transport to a dude ranch at Marion, fifty miles to the west, and wondering if living in these great open spaces doesn't do something to the mind, when I hear the sound of a cow drawing up at the Arrivals area. For those who might not have heard a cow drawing up at an Arrivals area, I can only describe it as a long, defiant moo, ending on a strangely falsetto note. This may be because it doesn't in fact emanate from a cow, but from a long black Lincoln limousine with a pair of horns on the front which is heading straight for me. I try to appear unconcerned, but the limousine moos again, more confidently this time, as if the damn thing has recognised me. And it has. A window slides down and a wide-brimmed black hat appears, and beneath it a woman's head which enquires politely if I'm Michael Palin.

Which is how I get to meet Ellen, better half of Leo; together they run the Hargrave Guest and Cattle Ranch – my home for the next couple of days.

Ellen is around my age, I would think, with a merry twinkle in the eye and a line in *Oklahoma!*-style skirts, cotton blouses and high-heeled boots, which is not an affectation for she comes from a family of nine children brought up in rural Kansas. One of her sisters, a slim blonde called Mary-Beth, is visiting and has been roped in to drive the limousine and pull the moo control every now and then.

Ellen and Leo Hargrave bought the 1400-acre ranch in 1968. It lies in a wide valley surrounded by distant mountains, an expanse of peacefulness, but not total isolation. There's a micro-brewery across the meadow, with two private planes parked outside, and some buildings tucked in amongst the trees about a mile down the valley.

Leo Hargrave is in his eighties, a good bit older and a good bit shorter than his wife. He has a similar mischievous twinkle in the eye which suggests that he doesn't take everything too seriously, but a compact, wiry body and well-worn dusty jeans suggest that he's dead serious about the farm. The fact that a man who flew missions for the USAF in the closing years of the Second World War should still be a working farmer seems to infect all us dudes and even as the first awkward introductions are made you can already feel city cares sliding off shoulders.

The word 'dude' may be politely taken to mean a guest but it also implies a non-Westerner, an urban American who wants to sample the Wild West without getting too wild. The age of the computer seems only to have increased the appeal of the cowboy, and many of my fellow-guests picked Hargrave Ranch off the Internet. For Leo and Ellen the dudes are not just a casual sideline, they're an economic necessity at a time when relatively small, traditional, environmentally friendly farms like theirs find it hard to fight the big boys.

So we can all take comfort: Dawn the attorney from Buffalo;

Smokey from Virginia, who's very proud of working in the cleanest coal-fired power station in the USA; John and Lynne from New Jersey; Chris, a grandmother from Massachusetts, and her three girlfriends, who are spending a week away from their men. We may look helpless, but they need us.

I'm soon confronting my incompetence with a bit of lasso-training from Ken, the ropeman. He's thin and wiry and what you can see of his face beneath the brim of his hat is lined and weathered. With enormous patience he stands by as I try to spin, throw and drop my rope clean over a black plastic cow's head stuck on the end of a wooden frame about fifteen feet away.

At my first attempt I'm slightly off target and lasso Nigel, the cameraman. I dissolve into uncontrolled peals of urban laughter. (We've been on the road a long time now, and hysteria lurks close to the surface.) Ken smiles politely but I think he finds my behaviour more alarming than that of any rogue steer.

The American West, rather like Ernest Hemingway, has passed from reality, through legend, to cliché. The Native American tribes have been whittled away, the herds of bison have gone, and the survivor, the cowboy, has been hunted down by film producers and advertisers and designers and graphic artists so it's hard to know what the real thing is any more.

I think of this as I find myself in the saddle – never a comfortable place for me – on a Palomino stallion called Pal, heading slowly out across long, green grass to which the morning mist still clings, behind Randy, the sort of cowboy Marlboro' would die for. He's lean, which pretty much goes with the job – cowboys seem to be conspicuously thinner than the rest of America – laconic and laid-back. Randy's introductory remarks in the paddock featured good sense rather than dire warning, and formal horsemanship was emphasised less than doing what comes naturally.

I've always had a mild aversion to being lifted off the ground (maybe my father dropped me when young) and I would unhesitatingly nominate the camel as my least favourite method of transport, but today, less than an hour after swinging on to the broad back of this distinctive pale tan horse, I'm not only trotting along like Roy Rogers, but I'm about to do a real cowboy's job.

The Hargrave Ranch is a working farm with 320 head of cattle. Some of them are loose and we're on our way to round them up. We've been told how to make the horse turn left or right, and stop, but it seems a bit of a leap from this to rounding-up. We enter a wooded area full of young pine and as Pal concentrates on picking his way through a web of fallen trees, I concentrate on keeping my hat on and my eyeballs in as the branches flick viciously at my face.

Everyone's still a little nervous when Randy shouts that he's seen the errant cattle.

'Michael, take the right and bring 'em round off the bank of that stream.'

Oh yes, thanks. Thanks a lot.

Of course I've done this many times, usually on my bicycle after seeing a John Wayne movie. Now that I'm actually on a real horse with real cows in the real West everything looks a little different. What the hell do I do if the beasts head straight for me, get out of control, or, enraged by a mosquito bite, start a stampede?

I needn't have worried. The rebellious cattle number fewer than twenty, of which eight or nine are white, fluffy calves and the rest either nursing mothers or several months pregnant. It's hardly a round-up, more like chasing a crèche. The attorney from Buffalo takes a tumble during the slow chase back through the pine woods, but on the whole, this bit of cattle action has an electrifying effect on the party. Having to ride instinctively, without thinking about riding, has calmed the nerves and turned us all into swaggering cowboys. Rick, here to celebrate his second wedding anniversary, was, like me, a quivering jelly two hours earlier, now he moves through the trees like a professional, occasionally shouting, 'Come on, cattle!' Or more threateningly, 'Hey! Cattle!'

Evening. Exhausted. At an open-air dinner beneath a big, protective river willow tree outside the old wood farmhouse, moments like the attorney's fall grow in the retelling, along with those of my Laurel and Hardy-esque attempts later in the day to rebuild a pine-log fence with the help of two grandmothers from Massachusetts.

Over a good country meal of prime beef, with cabbage, mushrooms, jacket potatoes of exceptional flavour, cream, fresh-baked bread and a Cabernet Sauvignon riskily called 'Dynamite', Ellen draws out the guests with well-practised skill. Part schoolmistress, part ringmaster, part entertainer, she soon has us all recounting wedding stories and how we met stories, and Rick is telling us about romance in a Laundromat and soon personal hygiene secrets are being traded as if we'd known each other from school. This would surely have had Hemingway running for cover. He came to the dude ranches of the West to get away from people, to recharge the batteries, hunt, fish and write. And it seemed to work. On his first visit to Wyoming in 1928 he completed the first draft of *A Farewell to Arms*, though he was to change the ending forty-eight times before he was satisfied. Two years later, with *A Farewell to Arms* a firm bestseller, he was at the L-Bar-T ranch working on *Death in the Afternoon* and writing to his friend Henry Strater 'Am going damned well on my book – page 174 – I can shoot the Springfield as well as a shotgun now.'

He never lost his fondness for the wide open spaces, though increasing fame made it more difficult for him to find the privacy he needed, which is perhaps why, in 1939, he agreed to be one of the first celebrity guests at the Sun Valley resort in the Sawtooth mountains of Idaho, newly opened by Averell Harriman, owner of the Union Pacific Railroad. In exchange for free accommodation and the odd publicity photo calls, he would be left alone.

As we sit around the camp-fire listening to the jolly gurgling yodels of 'The Singing Cowboy' I try to envisage Ernest wrestling with the problems of true declarative sentences to the accompaniment of 'Home, Home on the Range' and I realise why he was tempted to take the rich man's shilling and head for Sun Valley.

We leave the Hargrave Ranch with some regrets. Ellen and Leo are remarkable hosts, independent-minded and full of strong opinions; they seem truly happy here doing things their way, caring a lot for the land and not a fig for convention. They laugh a great deal, tell good stories and seem able to charm the most up-tight urbanite. For what it's worth I think Hemingway would have liked them. Who knows, they might even have persuaded him to join in with a verse of 'Happy Trails' after a good day's bear-shooting.

Sun Valley lies nearly four hundred miles due south of the Hargrave Ranch, where the big skies of Montana give way to the steeper valleys of Idaho, the potato state. Hemingway's accommodation at the Sun Valley Lodge, Parlor Suite 206, can be obtained for $389. All mod cons and handy for the tennis courts where, as the Second World War broke out in Europe, he and his soon-to-be third wife Martha Gellhorn took on

Mr and Mrs Gary Cooper.

I'm more interested in the later years when, for a short while, Hemingway made Idaho his permanent home. So I drive on past the tennis courts and the expensive cabins and into the nearby town of Ketchum.

Along the side of the road runs the old railway track that brought tourist prosperity to this small mining town. Now it's tarmacked. Today's car-bound tourists jog and cycle along it. A few of its elegantly curved steel bridges survive, and in the town itself remnants of the old red-brick, heavily corniced main street architecture can be found scattered amongst the new shopping malls and the park-and-ride schemes. Hemingway's old haunts, like the Casino Bar and Christiania's Restaurant (where he ate the night before his death) co-exist alongside boutiques like 'Shabby Chic Fabrics' and 'Expressions In Gold,' which would have had him turning in his grave.

Despite the amiable prettiness of Ketchum this is a melancholy place for the Hemingway follower, inextricably caught up with his final years, when, forced to leave Cuba by ill-health and political change, he came to live with Mary in an isolated house at the north end of town. I search for the house, down Warm Springs Road and right on East Canyon Run, without really wanting to find it. Throughout this journey I've driven up Hemingway driveways and knocked on Hemingway doors with a certain spring in my step, as if some of the man's energy and buoyancy were keeping me going. Now I'm at the simple pine-bark arch which marks the edge of his last property, lifting the chain that's slung across the road, knowing that I can no longer pretend that my travelling companion is immortal.

The man who lived here at 400 East Canyon Run was prematurely old, forgetful, paranoid and often desperately unhappy. At the end he believed FBI agents were tailing him (he thought he saw two of them sitting in Christiania's restaurant the night before he died). He attempted suicide with almost comical persistence, grabbing at shotguns whenever the opportunity arose. He was anxious about money and pathetically dependent on his wife Mary. This house is not a place where the tragedy of his life can be avoided or glossed over. Which makes it, in a way, more important than any of the others.

It is practical rather than beautiful, tucked into a gentle hillside overlooking the stony course of the Big Wood River. Across the river and through the trees is the highway that runs north to the dramatically rising peaks of the Sawtooth range. It's known as the Topping House (ironically) after the architect of the Sun Valley Lodge, who designed this in the same style, with walls of concrete poured into wood moulds, giving a first impression of a superior log cabin, but in fact being something much stronger. It was built in the 1930s, 'above the floodplain, unlike those new ones across the river', remarks our guide, Trish, pointedly.

Trish has let us into the house which is owned by the Nature Conservancy and not open to the public. Since Mary Hemingway's death in 1986 it has been maintained, like other Hemingway houses, in the way it was when he lived here. Apart from allowing us access, the Nature Conservancy are happy for me to be filmed spending the last night of my journey here. I know, as soon as I enter the house, there is no question of my doing that.

To someone who has spent ten months of the past year recreating Hemingway's life it's bound to come as a bit of a shock to be faced with the place where that life ended, but I feel something more than shock. Just as the sitting-room in his house in Havana gave me the feeling that he and his friends had only just left, so I find myself inside his house in Ketchum, standing in the eight- by five-foot porch-way where he shot himself as if it had just happened and I were the first man on the scene.

Yet it is nothing special, a perfectly ordinary entrance to a house, the sort of place where you slip off your hiking boots or muddy shoes, calling for a cup of tea after a long walk. It has a light brown lino floor, a small window with wild flowers in a jar on the sill. The crew are passing in and out, bringing the gear up the stairs from the garden. But I can't stop my imagination reminding me, with indecent vividness, of the final moments of Ernest Hemingway, raked over and repeated in all the biographies.

Seven o'clock on a perfect summer Sunday in July 1961. Hemingway, always an early riser, comes down the stairs (there they are – to the right of the fireplace behind me), and crosses the room to the kitchen. Does he ignore or enjoy the wide and wonderful panorama of river, trees and mountains beyond, which he couldn't fail to have seen through the picture windows? Stepping up into the kitchen (I can hear his freezer humming from where I stand), he found the key to the gun room, selected a double-barrelled Boss shotgun, loaded two shells, walked through to where I'm now standing, turned the gun on himself and, somehow, fired both barrels into his head.

Blood, death and appalling injury would not have shocked Hemingway. He had been shooting living creatures since he was a boy, he'd seen men blasted apart by mortar shells before his eighteenth birthday, he'd wiped out lions and leopard and rhino, and seen the horns of a bull pass through a man's thigh.

What terrified him most was not losing his life but losing his mind. Losing the ability to write. One of the saddest memories in this heart-breaking house must be that recalled by his doctor George Saviers, of Hemingway, the Nobel Prize-winner, breaking down in tears when he found himself unable to find words to compose a simple message for President Kennedy's inauguration in February 1961.

I'm glad to finish the filming and leave behind this house with photos of Ernest and Mary in happy times and bathroom towels marked 'Mama' and 'Papa', and the shelves of books and racks of period magazines and the inevitable African game trophies on the walls. Two distinctive memories will always vaguely disturb me though. One is a lustily gruesome painting above the stairs of two Spanish abattoir workers in the act of skinning a bull; the other, two small boxes carefully preserved in a glass display-cabinet in the sitting-room. One contains 5 mm cartridges, the other .22 rifle bullets.

Next morning. It's a beautiful July Sunday in Ketchum cemetery, on the far side of the Big Wood River from the house. It's a small cemetery, whose wrought-iron gates offer the only touch of flamboyance. The graves are modest, some marked by nothing more than a metal tag with a single word inscription – 'Baby' or 'Unknown'. The well-trimmed grass around them has been cut from the wild sagebrush scrub that covers the foothills behind and would, if it were allowed, push its way through the fence and reclaim the cemetery. This is still a hard land to live in.

The best way to find the plain marble tombstones of Mary and Ernest Hemingway is to look for the three tall spruce trees that stand above them. Around the horizontal grey slabs many other graves bear familiar names. His grand-daughter Margaux (spelt 'Margot' on her gravestone), also took her own life and her epitaph, 'A free spirit freed', could almost be his as well. George Saviers, Hemingway's doctor, lies a few yards away, and beside him the grave of his son Frederick Saviers, who died of a viral heart disease at the age of sixteen. One of

Ernest Hemingway's last letters was to this boy. Hemingway was having treatment at the Mayo Clinic in Rochester when he heard Saviers' son was ill but still found time, on 15 June 1961, to write him a cheery letter. It ended:

'Best always to you, old timer from your good friend who misses you very much.'

Not a bad way to sum up my feelings about this journey and the man whose footsteps I have followed from Oak Park to this graveyard in Ketchum – Ernest Miller Hemingway, July 21, 1899–July 2, 1961.

Hemingway's Life

short story collection) published.

1928 Leaves Paris, rents house in Key West. Second son Patrick born. Father commits suicide. Starts writing *A Farewell to Arms* in Key West and in various ranches in Wyoming.

1929 *A Farewell to Arms* published.

1930 Working on *Death in the Afternoon* – the bullfighting bible – in Key West and also up at the L-Bar-T Ranch, Wyoming.

1931 Buys house in Key West. Third son Gregory born.

1932 *Death in the Afternoon* published.

1933 *Winner Take Nothing* published.
First safari to Africa.

1935 *Green Hills of Africa* – first book about Africa.

1936 Working on *To Have and Have Not* in Wyoming, Cuba and Key West.

1937 *To Have and Have Not* published. Involved with Loyalists in Spanish Civil War, helps produce propaganda film *Spanish Earth*.

1938 *The Fifth Column* – play about the Spanish Civil War – and *The First 49 Stories* published.

1939 Separates from Pauline, starts living in Cuba with Martha Gellhorn. Writing *For Whom the Bell Tolls* in Paris, Cuba, Key West, Wyoming and Sun Valley, Idaho.

1940 *For Whom the Bell Tolls* published. Marries Martha Gellhorn. They set up home in Cuba at the Finca Vigía.

1941 He and Martha visit China and the Far East as foreign correspondents.

1942 Arms his boat *Pilar* to search for German submarines in Caribbean waters.

1944 War correspondent for *Collier's* magazine. Flies with RAF and helps liberate Paris, especially the Ritz wine cellars. Gathers material for *Islands in the Stream* (published 1970).

1945 Divorces Martha.

1946 Marries Mary Welsh. They settle back in Cuba.

1948   Visits Europe. Falls for Adriana Ivancic in Venice.

1949   Starts writing *Across the River and into the Trees*. Begins writing what was to become *The Garden of Eden* (published 1986).

1950   *Across the River and into the Trees* published. First really unfavourable reviews. Finally starts *The Old Man and the Sea* and continues with *Islands in the Stream*.

1952   *The Old Man and the Sea* is published and his reputation is redeemed.

1953   *The Old Man and the Sea* awarded Pulitzer Prize.

1954   January: Premature obituaries following two plane crashes within three days in northern Uganda. October: Awarded Nobel Prize for Literature.

1955   Starts writing African journal, to be published 44 years later as *True at First Light*.

1956   Old diaries discovered at the Paris Ritz which form the basis for *A Moveable Feast*, finally published in 1964.

1958   Moves out of Cuba and back to the American West, renting a cabin in Ketchum, Idaho.

1959   A 10,000-word article following the Ordonez-Dominguin *mano a mano* bullfights in Spain, later published in *Life* magazine (1960) and as the book *The Dangerous Summer* (published 1985). July: Celebration of 60th birthday in Málaga.

1960   Two suicide attempts. Treated at the Mayo Clinic with electric shock therapy.

1961   Discharged in January. Another suicide attempt in April, returns to clinic. Discharged as 'cured' 26 June. 2 July kills himself. Buried in Ketchum cemetery.

Acknowledgements

The Hemingway Adventure would not have been possible without the help of many people.

Martha Wailes was one of the first to come on board and her enthusiasm and exhaustive thoroughness in picking through the rich detail of Hemingway's life has helped make this book possible. As producer of the series, she showed indefatigable energy in organising, chivvying and cajoling people into helping us. Mirabel Brook guided us round the world with a steady hand and she and Laura Tutt turned a complicated shooting schedule into a precision instrument.

My co-adventurers and assorted towers of strength were David Turnbull, director, bon viveur, and the man who coined our title, Nigel Meakin, cameraman and bull impersonator, Jay Jay Odedra, his assistant, and John Pritchard, who recorded every roar, squeal and explosion – and those were just my pieces to camera.

In every country we needed special advice and we would have been lost without the help of Ernesto Juan Castellanos in Cuba, Elizabeth Nash and Robert Misik in Spain, Diane Saccilotto and Dajna Annese in Italy, Françoise Jamet and Brian Ferinden in Paris, Richard Bonham in Kenya, Patrick and Samantha Moray in Uganda, Mary Perkins, Carli Reardon, Rita Brown in Key West and Brad Leech in Petoskey.

Back at base camp, enormous thanks to Martin Cooper for stitching the television series together, to Eddie Mirzoeff for keeping a paternal eye, to my assistants Anne Chamberlain and Anouchka Harrison for making sense of my ravings, to Emily Lodge for paying our bills and especially to Anne James at Prominent Television for her help and inspiration.

Any list of those who have made things easier for us must be headed by Michael Katakis, Literary Rights Manager for the Hemingway Family, who has been a generous source of encouragement from the very beginning. His combination of expert knowledge of the subject and wonderful cooking skills is unequalled. I should also like to thank Kris Hardin, Natalia Henderson, David Boardman, Steve Plotkin and James Hill at the Kennedy Library, Mike Diehl, Alf Tönnesson, Hans Tovoté, Dudley Clarke, Candace Eaton, Sherrie Levy and Suzanna Zsohar.

Last but not least my thanks to Michael Dover, my editor, for steering the book safely home, and to Basil Pao. He has travelled with me so often now that he won't believe any compliments, but without his fine photographs there would be no book.

Credits

Select Bibliography

Carlos Baker, *Ernest Hemingway: A Life Story* (Scribner's, 1969)

Denis Brian (ed.), *The True Gen* (Grove Press, 1988)

Anthony Burgess, *Ernest Hemingway* (Thames & Hudson, 1978)

Norberto Fuentes, *Hemingway in Cuba* (Lyle Stuart, 1984)

A.E. Hotchner, *Papa Hemingway* (Carroll & Graf, 1999)

Bernice Kert, *The Hemingway Women* (W.W. Norton, 1983)

H. Lea Lawrence, *Prowling Papa's Waters* (Longstreet Press, 1992)

Kenneth Lynn, *Hemingway* (Simon & Schuster, 1987)

James R. Mellow, *Hemingway, A Life Without Consequences* (Houghton Mifflin, 1992)

Jeffrey Meyers, *Hemingway* (Harcourt Brace, 1985)

Fernanda Pivano, *Hemingway* (Rusconi, 1985)

Michael Reynolds, *The Young Hemingway* (W.W. Norton, 1986)

Michael Reynolds, *Hemingway, The Paris Years* (W.W. Norton, 1989)

Michael Reynolds, *Hemingway: The Homecoming* (W.W. Norton, 1992)

Michael Reynolds, *Hemingway: The 1930s* (W.W. Norton, 1997)

Michael Reynolds, *Hemingway, The Final Years* (W.W. Norton, 1999)

Lillian Ross, *Portrait of Hemingway* (*The New Yorker*, 1950)

Arnold Samuelson, *With Hemingway: A Year in Key West and Cuba* (Random House, 1984)

We can't ever go back to old things or try and get the 'old kick' out of something or find things the way we remembered them. We have them as we remember them and they are fine and wonderful and we have to go on and have other things because the old things are nowhere except in our minds now.

Hemingway to Bill Horne, Paris 1923